Dancing on the Dumpster

Willie J

Jesus Hands Publishing

Willie J

He lifts the poor from the dust and the needy from the garbage dump.   Psalm 113:7

Dancing on the Dumpster is a story of how the Lord pulls us up out of the garbage of our past and dances with us on top of it.

Dancing on the Dumpster

In order to protect their privacy, names have been changed.

Scripture quotations marked *New Living Translation* are taken from the Holy Bible, *New Living Translation*, copyright ©1996. Used by permission of Tyndale House Publishers, Inc., Carol Stream, IL USA. All rights reserved

Scripture quotations marked *THE MESSAGE* are from *THE MESSAGE*. Copyright ©Eugene H. Peterson 1993, 1994, 1995, 1996, 2000, 2001, 2002. Used by permission of NavPress Publishing Group.

Edited by Lisa J Lickel

Cover Design by Cheri Herron. All rights reserved.

Photo credits: All photos courtesy of the author and Denise Lundy Photography. All rights reserved.

ISBN: 978-0-9904281-7-6

Library of Congress Control Number: 2014955123

Table of Contents

Acknowledgements

First and foremost I want to thank my Lord and Savior Jesus Christ for pursuing me and not letting go and never giving up on me. Lord, you revealed yourself to me, you drew me to you, and all I did was respond. I am so grateful for my relationship with you. It's the only one I know will last forever. I hope your suffering was not in vain for me.

I can't put a price tag on my friends Sherry and Tonya who stood by me through my embarrassing moments of overreactions to life. John and Frieda, who led me to Jesus, I can't believe you guys wanted to invest in my life. Thank you.

Thank you to my parents who gave me life. I'm sure you did the best with what you had to offer.

Dr. Stan and Aunt Bea, I can't thank you enough for not shaming me when I was acting like a child. You could have crushed me at a very vulnerable state and you chose to build me up.

Thanks to my nursing friends for standing beside me and helping me through nursing school. I love you guys.

Thanks to my husband for being a great provider and supporting us through all our endeavors.

Thanks to my son for just being you. I love you more than you can imagine. I want the very best for you. I have prayed for your future wife since you were one year old.

Thanks to my editor Lisa for wading through my rough copies. You asked hard questions which gave me the outside perspective I needed to write my story. You went above and beyond and answered all my questions, which were many.

Willie J

Dancing on the Dumpster
From the Author

Well, it's time to write a book. "Don't put off until tomorrow what can be done today" comes to mind as I am off work all day today. I have the Gaithers singing "The Alpha & Omega" on Youtube with the screen downsized where I can see their performance and write at the same time. I love to worship the Lord through worship music. I enjoy Casting Crowns, Michael Card, and Fernando Ortega. I love to sing out of the hymnal as well.

My serenity room is set up, ready for me to sit and write. We moved to this house in July of 2012. I planned for my office/serenity room to be a place where I can go and spend time with the Lord and write. I have a candle outside my door that is lit when I don't want to be interrupted. My husband works out of our home in his office on the main floor. My serenity room is on the second floor, with a bathroom right across the hall; convenient, as I drink about a gallon of water a day. I had the room painted with serenity in mind. The walls are a soft, soothing violet color. When I enter the room it gives me a sense of protection and a desire to curl up in the oversized, fluffy recliner/rocker and just sit there and feel God's presence.

On the wall beside the rocker there is a picture of Jesus holding a child about one year old. The child looks sad but peaceful. Jesus has his chin on her head and she is leaning into him as if she is tired and just glad to feel safe. Jesus has a sad look on his face as if he knows what she has been through and is so glad the little one allows him to hold her. This picture reflects my relationship with Jesus and when I saw it, it touched something deep in my soul. I felt Jesus was saying,.yes child I know, yes child I know, just come and rest, be still and know that I am God. I am sad for what happened to you and what I want is for you to allow me to hold you and heal you.

I have a cherry L-shaped desk in one corner, and on the other side of the room I have two cherry bookcases full of books from school and my years of seeking the Lord and his healing. Skeleton Dan (nicknamed), who I received in a box from my first online anatomy and physiology class, sits next to my desk to remind me of my long hard journey through nursing school. He has lost his right arm from the elbow down, the top of his head is loose and keeps falling off, and if he had a brain you would be able to see the longitudinal fissure separating the right from left side of the brain. His condition reflects how hard nursing school was for me.

As I sit here typing at my desk, I can look up on my wall and see my bachelor of science in nursing degree and graduation picture that was taken the day I crossed the stage. If I look to my right, I can see a picture of my sixty classmates who graduated with me in 2012. Behind me, next to my bookcases, hangs a lighted electric waterfall which sounds like a real waterfall with birds tweeting.

In the corner of the room next to my closet I've hung certificates such as my Dale Carnegie achievements, county spelling bee award, and my GED. I grew up Amish and was not allowed to go to high school; as a result, I joke that I went from eighth grade to nursing school.

In June, 1999, the Lord started a work in me that I did not know I needed. It lasted much longer and has been much harder than I ever dreamed it would be. I had asked the Lord to heal me and make me who he intended me to be before the world got ahold of me. **I made a commitment to do whatever it took to become the woman he intended me to be**.

Many times on that journey I wondered why I had been

so naïve to make such a commitment. I had no idea what I was committing to when I made such a bold statement. It may be very similar to a marriage commitment in which the couple does not know what they are committing to and then, when things get tough, as they always do, they wonder what they were thinking. But nothing good comes easy. Relationships take a lot of work, especially our walk with the Lord, which, by the way, is the only relationship that is guaranteed to last forever.

From June, 1999 to December of 2006 I was in and out of counseling, spending about three hours a day alone with the Lord in order to function. I read lots of books on my identity in Christ. I read the *Gospel According to Job, Abba's Child* by Brennan Manning and many more. I spent many hours writing and pouring out my heart to the Lord. The Lord carried me as a father would a child. I am currently trying to figure out my relationship with the Lord as a grown daughter to a father. I knew how to relate to him when I felt like a child, but now it's awkward. I am not sure who I am as an adult daughter. Each day I am surrendering and asking him to show me who I am and how I am to live in a way that would please him.

As I've gone through my healing from my painful past, I've always known that I would write a book. I've had many names for books, such as *Labor of the Heart, The Healing Process, The Grieving Process, Dancing On the Dumpster;* and then the options of how to write the book. Do I write it in third person and call it fiction because most people may never believe my story? Or do I write it in first person and write it as a memoir along with what I have learned? I have decided to do the latter. I am writing to all those who have experienced abuse and loss and need a refreshing wave of hope that there is more than the here and now.

There is life beyond the pain we experience here on

earth.

You are not alone.

Many people are and have gone before you and experienced much pain and survived. You and I will too. There is hope as we forgive those who have hurt us, just as the Lord has forgiven us. We must remember that we hurt people just as others hurt us. We are all really made from the same "stuff." The question is, do we repent, die to ourselves, and surrender to the Lord? Or are we our own, continuing to live out of our sinful nature? The fruit of repentance will be evident, leading to compassion and sorrow for those caught up in sin. The fruit of being our own will lead to an angry, judgmental, and cold heart.

I remember a truth the Lord showed me during the hardest part of my pain: **"The ones who abuse are in more pain than the one on whom the pain is inflicted."** The point is that being far from God is much more painful than sitting in his lap, allowing him to heal us. This truth is crucial to freedom.

I believe what Solomon said: "There is nothing new under the sun" (Ecclesiastes 1:9). When I look around, I can't help but think, what is the point of this life? People are born, they sin, some build churches and make a difference for Jesus, and others make a difference for the devil and do their best to hinder God's work. So what is this life all about? It would seem the battle of this world is fought in the souls of man. God's handiwork and who he loves the most—his people—are the very thing the devil tries to use to get to God.

If you want to make parents suffer, an evil man or woman will torture their child right in front of them while keeping the parent from interfering. We have all seen those movies or heard of such situations in real life. I have thought many times, one of the worst things that anyone could do to me is hurt my son while I'm watching and not be able to do anything about it. I am sure all parents would attest to the fact that they would rather be abused or suffer than watch their child suffer. My heart goes out to those who have had to watch their child suffer, if it be cancer, left in a burning house, or any other kind of direct evil.

Now, if you **only get one thing out of this book**, I would like you to imagine that God loves all of us as his children and he is grieved in a way that we will never understand. He longs to gather us in his arms like a mother hen who wants to gather her chicks (Matthew 23:37). He wants us to **let him heal us** by meeting each one of us where we are.

So what can I write about that will be new to anyone? I want to write about something that will make a difference and will not waste the reader's time. What can I write that will meet you where you are in your unique situation? My goal for this book is that anyone could pick it up and find hope, feel God's tender love, and know that he is trustworthy. Recognize that he wants to meet you where you are, like no one else can. There is no way that I could speak to everyone's specific situation, but the Lord can.

Right now I work at the hospital three days a week, about forty hours a week. My son is in high school and is involved with his own activities, so I am available for food and money. I spend a lot of time with my two dogs; they are my babies, now that my baby is in high school. My four-pound Maltese likes to curl up in my lap. My seven-year-old, six-pound mix between a Maltese and Yorkie, I call the Holy Spirit dog. I gave him this name because when my son was about ten he would be at home by himself for a little while after school and I would pray that our dog would have the Holy Spirit so my son would never feel alone. I believe the Lord answered my prayer.

I believe this because any time anyone raises his voice or gets upset, The Holy Spirit Dog starts shaking and slinks away. At times when I was alone and I was talking to other people and letting them have it, of course no one was there, but it felt good to get it out, I would look over and see our dog looking at me, scared and shaky. I felt the Holy Spirit was speaking to me. If our dog was hanging his head I needed to change my attitude.

All names have been changed in the story to protect their identities. *It is not important for the reader to know anyone's name; it's only important that the Name of the Lord is glorified and known. I ask that the reader focus on the healer which is the Lord, not on the ones who inflicted pain.*

The only unique things I have to share are my experiences and the perspective I gained from those experiences. So that is where I will begin. Please understand that what I write about is from my perspective and I am human, so it's important that you pray about anything before you take anyone's advice. I hope that in spite of my fallen nature you will be able to glean some hope and truth from my experiences. I pray that the Lord will give you, the reader, truth as you read my book.

Author: Willie J

Chapter One
Shocking News

If you are like me, you skip over the first section from the author and jump to the first chapter. I would ask that you please read about the author before you continue reading. Thank you for being interested in my life story.

In the heart of my healing, it was a typical day where I found myself in emotional pain that included body memories. There were no pictures in my mind of the event, just intense emotions of feeling dirty and body memories that made me feel like I was being raped.

As a protective mechanism, my brain had erased the picture of some of my traumas and left me with the emotions and the body memories. This made my healing process a matter of detective work. I wish the emotion would have been erased as well, but that was usually the only sign I had that something was amiss. I would feel an emotion that did not match the present day's event and I knew it was a memory. An example would be if someone was short with me and walked away, I became fixated on what I thought was their rejection of me and felt intense emotion that should not be felt for such a minor issue. I would tell myself this situation was not a big deal, but my emotions would not listen. I felt like a helpless observer of my overreactions, because I could not do anything to stop them.

Our brain is separated into two parts: the right and left hemisphere. The right side is the creative side and the left side holds our library. The right hemisphere holds memories that cannot be recalled. For example, you know how to eat, but you cannot recall how you learned to eat; this is stored in your right hemisphere. The left hemisphere holds our library which we draw from when we say something like, "Remember when we went to the mall?" etc.

The right hemisphere also holds all the emotions we ever experienced, but without pictures. I learned that right hemisphere memories were those that took place before the left hemisphere/library was formed at about age two.

The memories for me were intense with no pictures, just intense screaming emotion that one could not ignore.

I was taught by a helpful counselor that if my emotional response to a current situation seemed exaggerated or did not match the present day's event then I was probably experiencing a memory flashback and needed to pray. This is a very important concept. Let me give you an example from my own life. I had severe abandonment issues, so when people I had known for a short time would decide to break off their relationship with me I was absolutely devastated, as if they were a very close relative who rejected me.

The intense emotion made absolutely no sense to me, but once I understood through therapy that I was being triggered into the times when I felt abandoned by my mom, it made sense. The current issue was only triggering the real pain of my past and that pain was real, but not real today. This can be very confusing to all involved, but must be understood in order for healing to take place. We have to put our focus on the right problem.

Most generally, in my situation, the present day event was minuscule and not really the problem. The real culprit that needed my attention was the memory of the past that was being triggered. If I wasted my time on the present day event, I would receive no healing. But if I prayed and asked the Lord to show me what I was really dealing with, then he would show me and I could gain healing. After I prayed through the past memory, the present day situation no longer bothered me. This was a sure sign that truth was revealed and my heart had been restored.

If a person does not learn this concept of past triggers, he or she can overreact emotionally, make mountains out of molehills, and it can cause others to have no desire to be around him or her. This causes legitimate rejection and pain creating a cycle that feeds lies such as: I am unlovable; I am the problem. From personal experience I can also tell you it's humiliating to feel intense emotions and wonder what on God's green earth is wrong.

I have to admit one time my abandonment/rejection issues were so raw that when I was driving and a stoplight turned yellow right before I got there, I felt rejected. I actually felt a physical pain go through my chest and I felt sadness. This was obviously not something I did consciously, but it revealed to me just how emotionally unstable I had become.

I shared these facts with very few people. Frankly, I was embarrassed and scared because I could not control my reactions. Thank goodness these overreactions do not happen today.

So, on this particular day I was stuck in a body memory that felt dirty and disgusting and I could not get through it. I had no pictures in my mind associated with this feeling, but I felt like my body was being raped in the present, yet I was alone in the house.

I felt nauseated, like my body wanted to purge the feeling or memory, and yet I could not make that happen. It was draining my body and it was overwhelming as if it was happening in the present moment. I curled up in a ball and shouted, "Leave me alone, leave me alone!"

I snuggled up to the old blanket I had kept from my childhood. It was a raggedy blanket that all my siblings fought over. My family called it the "cool" blanket because it was made of material that was very cool. During the summer when it was hot and we had no air conditioning, this blanket was life to us. I, being the baby of the family, took it with me when I left home. Here I was, a wife and a mother, and I was still cuddling with it.

I received a small amount of relief by screaming, "Stop! Stop!" Finally, I picked up the phone and called my mother because I had a gut feeling if I talked to someone from my past that person might trigger the actual memory and then the Lord could bring truth to the lies and I could be healed from the memory. I knew I was not dirty, yet the dirtiness in my soul was so very real. I could not shower enough or soak in enough suds to take away the feeling of filth.

The reader must understand that although my parents were Amish they lived in my dad's boss's house, rent free. Since they did not own the house they could use the electricity and phone. So I called my mother and after a little chitchat I told her that I felt I was reliving some abuse from my past and I felt it had to do with a family member, but I couldn't quite put my finger on it.

Without hesitation, she responded nonchalantly, as if she remembered we had steak for dinner, "Oh, yes. I remember when you were eight we came home and you said [this family member] had done something sexual to you. [This person] was standing there and he said you wanted it and let him do it."

Of course my thoughts were racing as I tried to put the pieces together. She talked about it as if it was no big deal.

"Really?" I said. "Well, at least you didn't let us stay alone again, right?" To which she replied, "We had to get ready for your sister's wedding, so we left you with him the next night."

Immediately I knew what memory I was stuck in.

I cannot write about what happened that night. He hurt me one last time and told me he had given me a good thing and now he was going to leave me alone—and left me alone, he did. I was so lonely after that, I wished for the abuse again. This is a sad reality. In my childhood and on into adulthood, this abuse tainted my view of sexuality and caused me to struggle with my identity.

Mom continued, "Well, what was I supposed to do?" I had no response for her, I had received more than what I had expected to receive from the phone call. I don't remember the rest of the conversation. I somehow said good-bye without letting her know how I really felt.

I hung up the phone and sat in shock. Had I really just had that conversation with my mother? She did not even apologize or seem to think she had done anything wrong or that the incident was really anything to be upset about. Was I just making a big deal about nothing?

This is how my family made me feel most of the time when I questioned things throughout my childhood. They never did anything wrong, I was just overreacting to the situation. When my brother picked up my doll and held it just out of my reach and punched her face until her head fell off, my mom and sister, who were present in the room, laughed and did not try to stop him. I got upset and they laughed and said, "Oh it's just a doll."

Later, when I recounted this story to my third and final counselor, he verified that I responded to these situations the way a human being should respond. My family was the problem, not me. I wish I had known that back when I was little. I just assumed I was overreacting and my family was right. Little did I know that my family was desensitized to matters of the heart.

Before my mom told me this story I knew that she had emotionally aborted me, but to hear her so casually mention that she had not even thought about protecting me was a hard reality to face. What I learned from my mother that sad day matched what I was discovering in my memories as I spent time with the Lord and as I continued my weekly therapy.

As an adult, I would often cry about not feeling protected and I was not sure why that pain was so deep, but now it made more sense. I was eight years old when I had approached my mother hoping for protection from a teenaged family member, and instead I received more pain through her ambivalence. The loneliness and pain I had encountered in my memories now matched the story I just heard from my mother.

The above memory is an example of my brain erasing the picture of the memory and leaving me with only the emotions and the body memories. If my mother had not told me this story I would not know that I had approached her to ask for help. I still have no picture memory of this incident. I wonder how many more memories have been erased.

I soon learned as I was going through therapy that I only wanted to know what was needed for me to heal. I did not want to know anything about my past that was not necessary for me to become a better representative for Christ, but if I needed healing from trauma so I could be his hands and feet, then I wanted to do whatever it took to heal.

It's important to focus on the goal of healing from a painful past. The goal should always be to be a better you, not to soak in self-pity or bitterness and point fingers at those who hurt you.

The goal of healing is solely to be a better you for Jesus; anything else will just make you a more selfish, bitter, and angry person.

I hope my mother never saw how she emotionally aborted me; I don't know that she could handle the reality of what she did to me. I would never wish the truth upon her. I think she did the best with the knowledge she had. Now I simply want to be healed by the Lord and not carry any bitterness towards anyone. I must grieve the loss of my innocence and of not being protected, but the greater loss is for my mother who never got to love because she was too numb.

Chapter Two

Down through Generations

My parents were both raised in large Amish families of seven or eight siblings. Shame and control ruled both of their lives; love was absent, leaving a void in their hearts.

My mother was molested by a close family member and nothing was done to heal the shame in her life. She grew up in a home where her dad was angry and decided to leave the Amish church, but my grandma would not change her beliefs. Oddly enough my grandpa used to drop grandma off at the Amish church while he drove his car on to a Mennonite church. This brought a lot of shame to my mother and her entire family. Their family dynamics were odd for an Amish family. Divorce was never ever an option and so, no matter what my grandpa did, my grandma stayed with him. Grandma continued to dress in her Amish clothes yet she let grandpa drive her around in what was considered his worldly car.

The Amish do not have cars, electricity, phones or any electronic devices such as computers, TVs or radios. They sew their own clothes and do laundry with an old style washing machine run by a generator where clothes are fed through a wringer. They plant a large garden and use canning and freezing as a way to preserve their fruits and vegetables. They pick apples locally and can applesauce and buy their own cattle to butcher for meat. They limit their visits to the doctor and hospital to times when they're really sick.

Grandpa wired his house with electricity and grandma used it. Grandpa continued to wear Amish clothes while driving his car. It was confusing to me when he would come pick us up in a car to take us to their house, and yet Mom and Dad both told us we were not allowed to have a car and if we did they would never drive with us even though Dad used a car to go to work. The inconsistency of saying one thing and doing another was woven throughout my childhood. When I questioned these situations I was told to be quiet and that things were not the way they should be. This did not satisfy my questions.

Dad was very angry with my mother's mom and dad because he wanted to buy the family estate and Grandpa wanted too much money for it, according to Dad. Hindsight tells me that Grandpa did not want my dad taking care of my grandpa when he was old, so he raised the price knowing my dad would not buy.

Most Amish families have a tradition where the family estate is practically given to one of the children and then a smaller house called the "Daudy Haus" (translated Grandpa House) would be built on the same property and the elderly parents would live in the small house and one of the children would live in the bigger house with the expectation that the child and his/her family would take care of the parents. This tradition is set up so that the elderly need not be placed in a nursing home. This can be a beautiful thing where grandparents can see their grandchildren on a regular basis and share meals, time, and love.

If the child who chooses to move into the family estate is on good terms with his parents it can be a wonderful expression of love. However, it can also be a source of control, leading to anger and quarrels. My dad was not a man who surrendered control to anyone; neither was my grandpa, so, had we been chosen to get the family estate, it would have been disastrous.

My dad was a very angry man and he would randomly decide that Mom could not leave to go help her parents. This, in large part, was due to his anger over the estate. Sometimes Mom would sneak to see Grandma and Grandpa while Dad was working in the field. My dad worked for a non-Amish farmer, so he would drive his boss's car to work and use tractors and combines to cultivate and plant the fields.

Amish farmers were not allowed to use tractors and combines. They had to use horse-drawn cultivators and planters, and this process was long, hard labor and produced very little profit. My dad was allowed to enjoy all the "worldly" possessions without actually owning any of them. The same was true for our family because we lived in the house of my dad's boss and had electricity and a phone. This was a luxury for an Amish family.

At the ripe old age of seventy-seven and seventy-six, my mom and dad still live in the same house where I grew up. My dad is getting ready to retire and they will move to a house they bought many years ago. It has been sitting vacant, waiting. So, in their late seventies, my parents will start living in a house without electricity and a phone. I am very curious to see how this will work.

My sister is expected to take care of them, because she lives about a mile from where my parents will live. I am also anticipating how my sister and her family will handle having my parents live a mile away. My dad has his own way of doing things, and when he is crossed in any way he gets angry and the experience is less than endearing.

My dad errs on the side of extreme thriftiness; he does not mow his yard when it's the typical height. He waits until it reaches about eight inches so that he can cut it with a weed mower and use it to feed his horses; this saves him money on buying food for the horses. In the winter he sprays water on the outside of all the windows so it will seal the windows in hopes to decrease the electric bill.

During my childhood, if we wanted something out of the refrigerator during a meal we were not allowed to open the refrigerator to get it. The refrigerator should be opened once right before a meal and then once after the meal so that the refrigerator wouldn't have to work harder and therefore use more electricity. Dad placed a plastic wrap around the table legs to keep the heater from blowing heat towards the refrigerator, once again causing the refrigerator to use more electricity. Yes, you guessed it, to save money.

We couldn't wait until Dad left for the day so we could turn the bright lights on. In spite of having electricity we did not get to use it like we wanted to. In the kitchen we had a forty-five watt bulb; behind it was a mirror so that it would reflect more light. When Dad was gone we would use the bright fluorescent lights that were right next to the small bulb.

One day my dad was mad because he was sure I had my fan on high and he wanted me to keep it on low. I had a deadbolt on my bedroom door. It did not stop my dad, and he broke down my door in order to make sure I had the fan on low. I was very scared; I did not think he would actually go to such lengths to make sure my fan was on low. My dad had, and still has, deep-seated anger and control issues. Throughout my seventeen years of living under the same roof as my dad I heard him threaten to kill everyone in our household and many others in the community. He was a loan shark to the Amish and when they would not pay, he would often threaten to burn their house down and hope they were in it. I learned to stay out of the way, so he never threatened to kill me.

Once I heard my father tell my brother that he hoped he

would be in a car wreck and die instantly. When my father was a teenager, he was angry with his parents and he burned down their barn.

I don't know too much about my dad's parents. Once again my dad controlled us to a point where he told my mom when she could go see his parents. He did not allow her to leave unless the task list was caught up at home and if it didn't cost too much. One great thing that came out of my dad's stinginess was that, instead of a horse and buggy, I was given a bicycle to ride. I loved riding my bike and I could go further, faster, on my bike. I felt I had some independence when I got on my bike.

I could ride a hundred miles in a day if I needed to. At times my mom would want me to go to the store for her. The closest store was seven miles away. Sometimes I would get back from the store and she would forget something and I had to go back. I loved it. I felt free when I was out on my bike and I was fast. I always tried to beat my best time and see if I could get Mom to say, "Good job! That was fast."

Nope! Never received an "atta girl," or a "thank you." Later in life when I asked Mom why she was so stingy with her compliments, she stated adamantly that I should know that I did a good job if she didn't say anything. Her idea was that she would make me a proud person if she gave me compliments. I guess she had a purpose behind withholding compliments. According to her perspective I should be a real humble person. I am sorry to inform you that I have just as much pride as the next person.

One thing I do know about my dad's growing up years was that they were made fun of by the Amish community. I guess they were considered odd. I know my dad was odd, but I don't know about the rest of the family. They were called the "goats" and this followed my dad, especially because he was not popular. So this carried on to our family and I was called a goat and made fun of when I was out among the Amish community.

I didn't like telling people who my parents were because as soon as they found out, their countenance changed, and they nodded as if they had just found out everything they needed to know about me. It made me sick as I saw their attitude change towards me; they had a look of complete repulsion. Prior to their knowledge of who my parents were they treated me with respect, but as soon as they found out, they said "Oh!" like they just made a great discovery. They would get that look of disgust on their face.

I grew up having to prove that I was worthy of kindness or respect. I never had a chance to have a clean slate with the Amish community; my slate was dirty just because of who my parents were and I had to prove that I was not like my dad. This caused a lot of unnecessary striving on my part. Now I know that I'm worthy because of who I am in the Lord, not because of who my parents are or are not, or what I do or don't do.

I must admit that in spite of knowing the truth about who I am as a child of God, I still struggle with the way the Amish viewed me. It branded shame on the slate of my heart and it has most definitely left a scar.

My default mode is to remember the identity I grew up with. It takes effort for me to remember my identity in Christ. Today, if I am made fun of or someone rejects or shames me, my automatic default mode reverts to the old thinking. I start to think maybe the people of my past were right, I am not lovable. But then I must remember that is my default thinking and to take it captive and remind myself of what the Lord says about me. I am valuable to the Lord because he made me.

The Amish community would make fun of me and I would pretend it didn't bother me. However, when I arrived home and I sat alone in my room, emptiness and sadness would consume me. I could not cry; instead I would stare out of my second story bedroom window, gazing at the fields that went on forever, wondering why was I so bad that my family was repulsed by me and now the community didn't like me either.

I couldn't understand what I had done so wrong. If there was nothing that proved something was wrong with me, I was bad and wrong because I had been born. No one needed more of a reason than the fact that I was born to be made fun of. My family used to look down their noses at me and with contempt they would ask, "What do you want now?" If I was upset the response was, "Oh, it's just little Miss Crybaby." I don't think my family realized the message they were sending me; I was just born at a time where my family's minds were preoccupied with other things and another child was an annoyance. My questions and my tears annoyed them.

My biggest mistake was that I had been born. I wondered, did I ask to be born? Why were others mad at me for existing? I always tried so hard to be perfect but even then I was found guilty. I thought if I actually did something wrong, what punishment would be in store for me?

Throughout my childhood years I fluctuated between wanting to be left alone and then feeling so lonely that I would long for abusive words or actions rather than have no interaction with others. This struggle followed me into adulthood and led to many unhealthy relationships. If people feel they don't exist they will seek out anyone and anything to chase this feeling of loneliness. This answers the question many people ask: "Why does he/she stay in an abusive relationship?"

As a child I was not given a chance to be accepted as me. Later on I will write about my life when I left the Amish community, but I want to add here that it was hard for me to understand that people actually liked me when I went out into the world. I was baffled; this was a brand new experience for me. I could meet people who were not Amish and they smiled at me and appeared to like me. Amish people never liked me when they first met me and found out who I was related to.

Truth is, people treat others the way they do because of who they are, not because of who others are. So, in other words, if I treat someone with disrespect, it says more about me than it does the person I am disrespecting.

Our Lord Jesus Christ saved us because he is good, not because we are good. This is the principle that I'm trying to explain in the above paragraph.

Chapter 3

In the Beginning

As I was going through therapy and trying to make sense out of the deep emotional pain I carried in my soul, I would ask Mom questions about my childhood. She shared that I was not planned. Dad was very angry when he found out she was pregnant with me. Dad wanted only two children and they already had three. I was five years behind my brother; neither one of us were planned.

Mom shared that Dad would yell at her throughout her pregnancy and she would plead with him to stop because she could not handle the yelling while she was pregnant. I asked Mom why he was yelling and she really didn't know except to say it was his regular practice to be upset about his job or people in the Amish community. Either way, she was not as strong when she was pregnant and she begged him to stop yelling because it would make her cry and the more she cried, the madder Dad got.

Mom was thirty-five when she was pregnant with me. My brother Caleb was a hellion. Mom told me many stories about how hard it was to control him. Caleb would put his feet outside of the playpen and move the entire playpen across the floor and start tearing wallpaper off the wall. Mom admitted she was scared of Caleb and was at her wit's end with him.

Between Dad and Caleb, Mom was completely exhausted emotionally. She had nothing left to offer an infant. Mom said that I cried all the time and Dad would yell and tell them to take the baby into the bedroom and shut it up. I inquired how they got me to stop crying and she said they "just shook me until I stopped crying."

My brother Caleb shared his perspective of my birth into this world. He said, "Dad was fine until you were born. You cried all the time and so Dad was mad and no longer gave me swing rides." My brother shared this perspective when we were both adults. His five-year-old memory of my birth was basically that I ruined our dad. Dad had to yell because I was such an awful baby.

Often, when I would hear stories from my family like the ones above, it would match the emptiness I felt inside. Through my therapy I would encounter feelings of complete unworthiness and I could not shake the feelings. I felt I was never invited to exist. I felt I had to pay a price to be born. I had to prove I was worthy of being born. Everyone else on the earth had a right to be here, but I felt I needed to prove that I was worthy to exist. Why did I feel this way?

From what I have studied about the brain, the stress of a crying baby and a screaming dad would have resulted in negative non-verbal messages as I was being held. I do think that my mom and sister loved me and I think Dad did as well, but the crying he could not tolerate. Obviously this was not my fault as it was an issue in my dad, but it left me feeling empty and lifeless. I did not feel I was the sparkle in anyone's eye.

One of the things I learned in reading the book *Living from the Heart Jesus Gave You* was that the only thing that motivates a child is being the sparkle in someone's eye. The only thing a child will seek out is that person who smiles at them and gives them a feeling of being the apple of her eye. This is crucial to a child's life. I did not have this and later, as an adult, I would stay in abusive relationships because *I felt lucky if ANYONE wanted to be with me.* I was still looking to be that sparkle in someone's eye. I desperately wanted to be special to someone, anyone.

My sister was twelve years older than me and I know she wanted me to be born. However, I am going to guess that because the family struggled with my crying and Dad's anger about my crying, I was probably not comforted when I was being held. Their focus was to keep me from crying so that Dad would not get mad. The tension in the home was felt deeply by my little crying soul.

Through my later years of healing I encountered memories where I just cried and cried and I could find no comfort. After I studied the brain and understood that the right hemisphere holds all the emotional memories without pictures of my first two years of life, I was pretty sure that I had felt all the tension from my family and there was no comfort. My mom struggled to keep it together and keep Dad appeased. My sister took on the role of trying to keep the peace.

I remember when I was older, my sister would rush us upstairs away from Dad when he would get angry. My sister would tell us to play cards. I had a hard time understanding why we were pretending nothing was wrong. Dad was downstairs threatening to kill people and Mom was crying, yet we were playing cards. I felt like we should be doing something, yet we continued to play Uno. This made me feel crazy because it didn't make sense in my mind.

There is the saying about the elephant in the room. Well, I would sum up my life with my family for the first seventeen years of my life as walking through elephant dung that was up to our knees and yet everyone acted as if nothing was wrong. I saw the elephant dung and I would ask questions about what seemed obviously wrong to me. Yet, the rest of the family just kept acting like the elephant dung was not there even while they reached down to get their boots unstuck from the elephant dung.

My family continued to go through the motions and pretended things were okay. This may be why I can't stand to *not* talk about problems I have with my husband or my family now. I absolutely cannot tolerate pretending we are not upset if something is wrong. We must talk about the elephant in the room, if there is one.

The tension in my childhood was probably the cause of my cognitive dissonance, which means what one side of my brain thinks does not match what the other side feels. For example, my right side of the brain holds my feeling of emptiness, worthlessness, abandonment, and unlovability. My left side of my brain, the logical side, thinks, "Why am I feeling like this? I learned about my identity in Christ and I believed it. I knew that things were not the way they should have been in my childhood, but I knew my parents had done the best they could and I wanted to move on and not be affected by my past." However, my right side, my feeling side of my brain, would not let me forget how I felt. It was frustrating, the logic part of my brain thought it was a waste of time to feel my past.

One member of our family was very mean to me throughout our childhood. He made me believe that I was special and he invited me into the barn and told me not to tell anyone. He would place me on my head while he molested me. We would also play cards on his bed and then he would proceed to touch me inappropriately. When I was eight I realized this was not right and pushed him away. This was also when I told Mom what he was doing and Mom left me alone with him again, and he hurt me one last time. This person made me feel that he was offering something good to me and then he was going to leave me alone.

Let me insert here that *I did not remember this sexual*

abuse until I was eighteen years old and falling in love with a man who became my husband. The brain is a powerful tool; it can help you remove memories that are too hard to handle. The brain, when under severe trauma, can actually erase the picture of a memory, leaving the person with only the emotions. I described this in the first chapter where my mother told me that I had shared that a family member was abusing me. I have no memory of telling her, but I do have body and emotional memories of what happened after I told her.

In other abusive family situations I recall, my brother Caleb would take me on sled rides in the snow and dump me off into the snow. I would go crying to Mom and she would just tell me to stay away from him. She would not try to punish him because she knew it would have no effect. Caleb knew Mom would not protect me and so he did whatever he wanted to me. He was the only person I had to play with so I would eventually return to him and ask for more sled rides, and the outcome was always the same, I would get dumped in the snow purposefully and Caleb would laugh. Caleb knew that he would not get in trouble.

When I was older, Caleb pulled out my chair when I was going to sit down and I fell on the hard linoleum floor. I am pretty sure I broke my tailbone because my tailbone is a funky shape now.

I was desperate to have someone to play with and since Caleb was the only one around, I hoped every time he would be different. He never was. My mom would go off into her own little world as soon as Dad left the house. My sister and my older brother worked, so I was left alone. I was so alone that I chose abuse over loneliness. This pattern continued into my adult life. The childlike hope that maybe this time the person who hurt me would be different also followed me into adulthood. I always wanted to believe a bad situation was going to be different the next day and the next. This cycle is sad in childhood, but to know that I continued this cycle well into adulthood is even sadder to me. The cycle did not stop until my last and final counselor showed me an example of a healthy relationship. Once I had an example, I could change the cycle.

It's important to note here that I so longed to be special to someone that I would pursue anyone who showed even slight interest in wanting to be with me. As an adult I was still looking to be the apple of someone's eye. I also stayed in abusive relationships long after it was obvious that I should leave because I couldn't tolerate the pain I felt when a relationship ended. The pain felt like my heart was being ripped out and I relived the abandonment pain and detachment pain from my mother every time a relationship ended. So I didn't want any relationship to end.

As I am ready to enter my forties and I know my whole story, I have to ponder the question, "Shouldn't I have known better?" The point I am getting at is that we know only what we know and what we have experienced up to any particular moment. If most of us knew ten years ago what we know now, wouldn't life be different?

The problem is that we didn't know ten years ago what we all know now. For those of you who had a typical childhood and are now forty or more, aren't there many things that you think, "If only I would have known ten years ago what I know now?"

A wonderful, healthy person once told me life is like a spiral staircase, and as you climb this staircase you may encounter some of the same issues, but with a new, more mature perspective of life. All this is to say, no matter where we are on the continuum of life, if we are growing, all of us will say in ten years, "I thought I knew something ten years ago, but I knew nothing." If you are a product of an abusive childhood or are from a loving childhood, either way, I hope we are all able to say if only I knew then what I know now.

A wise man once said, "Regret is the price we pay for wisdom."

Chapter Four
Decision Making

On my fifth birthday I remember standing between two tall poles in my parents' front yard. These were big round telephone poles. One had a light on the top; the other connected the electrical lines to our house. I stood there on my fifth birthday and said to myself, "Willie, look around, do you see how bad it is now? Well, brace yourself, it's going to get a lot worse." This memory is not fuzzy; this is a solid memory I have had as long as I can remember. It was a pivotal memory, it was a decision I made that day to accept that *I was on my own to survive in this world.*

During my seven years of continuous therapy I had the pleasure of sitting for one week with a psychologist who was an expert on the neurology of the brain and understood how the presence of abuse and the absence of love affect the brain. I shared the above memory with him and he asked me if I realized that, at the age of five, children decide what life is all about.

He said, in essence, what you decided was that life was hard and no one was going to protect you so you were going to have to take care of yourself. I had to agree that this was exactly what I thought and felt. I had come to a conclusion that at the ripe old age of five I was on my own. The day I decided this I left a part of my heart behind and moved on without emotion.

In the psychology world the word for this is

"dissociation." I could not handle feeling anything in my little world and so I left my heart behind and moved on to become someone without the hindrance of emotions and pain. This is a tool that I believe God allows during severe trauma. I had no resources to deal with my pain and loneliness. Therefore, I left it behind and placed it in a file where I hoped it would never be opened again.

As I think of this scenario I marvel. How did I know at age five that my family life was bad and it wasn't going to get better? That thought process sounds way beyond that of a five-year-old. I am sure the Lord was with me and giving me wisdom even though I did not know him yet.

My dad was always in trouble with the Amish church. His anger would lead to an excuse to cut his beard. The Amish are supposed to let their beards grow without trimming them. My dad would trim his beard and say it was because he had been upset with one of us or someone in the community. Reality was that my dad wanted to look good for the women he encountered when he was out to eat with his boss. Every single day that my dad worked, his boss would take him out for lunch.

The reason I want to talk about this topic of my dad and the church is that many Amish preachers came to visit our home to try and reason with my dad. One of these preachers I really liked. I longed for him to take me home with him and I would look at him and think surely he realizes what is going on in our home? Can't he see all the evil in our home? He never took me home and he didn't make my dad change. Yet, each time he was there I hoped maybe this time something would change.

One time this preacher I liked decided to have everyone sit down with Dad and we were all supposed to share our hearts. Now that I'm older I can see that this preacher was really trying to open up communication in our family and help my dad. However, I wanted to be removed from the situation because it was not getting better. The preacher's idea was great for a normal human being, but my dad wanted nothing to do with anybody telling him how he had hurt us. I don't recall all the details, but I know Dad was madder after the fact than he was before the meeting.

Another time one of my dad's siblings heard what dad was doing and they called the authorities. The cops came out and took my dad away in handcuffs. I don't remember how old I was, but I remember feeling relieved. It wasn't long until he sweet-talked the psychiatrists and he was back in our home. I don't remember which incident led to his departure with the cops or which incident led to the preacher gathering us all together. All I can say is that when others got wind of some of the things Dad was doing they felt a need to get involved. Yet to this day my dad is still the same angry man he was so many years ago. I feel sorry for him; I can't imagine living with such anger. **I'm so very glad that Jesus chose to reach down and help me out of my pain so that I am not an angry person today.**

If you're wondering about the details of how my dad's anger played out in our family's life, just know it was not good if the cops were called and he was taken away. I don't think more needs to be said about that.

There are two types of trauma: the absence of necessary good things, and the presence of abuse (Wilder). I had the presence of abuse, but I also had the absence of necessary good things. One thing I hardly ever received was a "good job" or a compliment. I would try to work harder and faster in hopes that someone would notice and say "good job." No one seemed to notice; instead they simply had more work for me to do.

I received one compliment from my mom in the entire almost forty years of my life. From my perspective it came

25

with a motive to get me to be quiet, but it was still a compliment. I asked her why I couldn't wear makeup like the other girls in school. I went to a public school and noticed such things. She said I was pretty enough, I did not need makeup. Today, at almost forty, I wear very little makeup. I wonder if it's because of this compliment?

My dad was stingy with his money so we were given the opportunity to go to the local public school instead of going to the Amish private school. I am not sure the reason, but they didn't let me go to Kindergarten. I started first grade when I was five and going to be six in October. I absolutely loved school. I didn't feel the evil at school liked I felt at home and the kids usually liked me. It was hard for me to say no and so I would do my classmates' homework because I wanted to make sure they liked me. I was very smart and could get A's without even trying.

I was one out of three Amish students in my grade. We were respected. When I got up to bat during our softball games, everyone would chant, "Amish Power, Amish Power!" I was the only girl who could hit a home run. I did not get to play sports because I was Amish, but these games were during P.E. or at recess. I was very insecure and was never sure that anyone liked me, but my experience in school was much better than my experience at home and among the Amish.

Chapter Five
The Turning Point

My heart was pounding as the bus rolled to a screeching halt. My mind was racing, this was the last straw. How could my parents even think of taking away my right to succeed? I raced down the steps of the bus, my hands and my body shaking and trembling from anger. I felt the hot oil on the country road as it squished under my shoe; I hardly heard the gravel crunch as I raced up the driveway. We lived in an old, two-story, white, broken-down house with an open porch on the front. The paint was peeling and the gutters were rusted. I ran up the sidewalk that was full of cracks. Grass and weeds made it hard to see.

That day my life ended.

I reached for the old screen door and yanked it open. It creaked and banged behind me. I was fuming mad. I felt like my eyes were burning and my stomach was going to lose all that I had eaten in the last year. I noticed the inside porch door was closed. They usually close it when they leave. Surely they would not have the audacity to give me such news to deal with alone?

As I stood in the old kitchen, I remembered back to just a couple of hours earlier when my English teacher had called me out into the hallway. He had a look of anguish on his face, and I wondered if someone in my family had died. He had that serious of a look of tragedy all over his face. But I was not ready for what he said next.

"Willie, your parents called."

My heart pounded and skipped a beat. Now I was sure there had been a death.

"They said you can't go to the State Spelling Bee."

I felt like someone punched me in the gut. No, this can't be!! Now I suddenly wished they were all dead. How could they do this? I had worked so hard and won the School and the County Spelling Bee and was the only one to represent our county to go to the State Spelling Bee. I had been pacing the floor learning words I couldn't even pronounce. I had visions of going to Washington D.C. Now my dreams were all smashed.

My mouth dropped open and the questions started pouring out. "Why? Why didn't they tell me earlier? I've been studying every night, how can they take this achievement away from me, and who do they think they are? Will someone go in my place?"

Since my family was Amish I never got to do anything with the other kids at school. No music, no dramas, no sports. I was a great basketball player but never got to play except in P. E. Now this...

"But, Mr. Berry, can they do this? Do they have the right to do this to me?"

He slowly nodded his head. "Yes, they are your parents. They can withhold you from any activity."

"Why didn't they tell me themselves? Why would they call the school and make you tell me?"

Mr. Berry sadly shook his head. "I have never had to deal with this kind of thing. They said you could not be on TV and the State Spelling Bee is televised, so they can't allow you to go."

"So will someone else go in my place?"

"No," Mr. Berry said. "It's over for this year. We are out of the competition if you can't go."

I had never been in touch with anger and rejection and hurt like this before.

At home, as I looked around the kitchen and realized my parents were gone and I could not confront them. I was really mad. This was it, I told myself. "Everyone hates me anyway, so I'll teach them a lesson."

I called one of my friends from school and asked her mother to pick me up. I was running away! I was twelve years old and in eighth grade. I would find a way to make it. The thought about finishing school or getting a job or finding a way to live didn't matter to me at the moment. All I cared about was that I could not and would not stay in this house of hate. I would do whatever it took to never come back to this house and never see these people who called themselves my family.

The only thing I remembered taking with me was money. I was thinking rationally enough to consider that I needed money to live. So I stole all the money I could find in my parents' safe, $300.00. I left a note on the table that said, "You shouldn't have done it! I am leaving and I never want to see you again!" I left the note right where my dad would sit for dinner and I knew they would get it.

My friend's mom came and picked me up and took me to her house.

That was the day I decided I would not be Amish when I grew up. There was no way I could ever take an achievement away from my child such as the spelling bee, or anything else, for that matter. If being Amish meant me and my family could not excel in life, then forget it.

I could not believe my parents would crush the hope and dream I had of going to Washington D.C. Their words and actions never matched. Their excuses for doing or not doing certain things were because they needed to obey the church/God. Yet, my dad would yell and threaten to kill people who did not pay him the money they owed him. He threatened to kill everyone in our household except for me. The only reason he did not make such threats to me is because I learned how to stay out of his way. I am sure we have all thought things such as "I wish he were dead," but to say them and then spell it out to the point of saying how you want them to die? That was psychotic.

So, after seeing and hearing such heinous attitudes and actions now they want to obey the church/God? Really? I decided that if God was Amish, I sure wanted nothing to do with him because it sounded more like hell.

Looking back, I now realize my parents were doing all those things to look good; it was so that they would not get in trouble with the church and be exposed in front of the congregation. In the Amish church, when someone is found to be doing something wrong according to their rules, that person is shamed in front of the whole congregation. This is done to motivate that person to never do that wrong thing again. The result was that people live in fear and feel controlled by the church.

From what I have learned about our Lord's character, he does not control his children; rather, he allows us to make our own choices. So when my parents decided I could not go to the State Spelling Bee, they were not thinking of me. They were thinking of how they would look if they got in trouble, and that was all that mattered. When I ran away they did whatever it took to keep me at home and keep me under wraps because they did not want other families to know their child had run away. They did not really care about my welfare; it was more about what they looked like to others. Their number one concern was what the church thought.

Now that I'm an adult, I ask, "Where was God in this spelling bee incident?" I think he was calling me out of the Amish, revealing to me that I could never live under such controlling evil. He knew that it would take something this close to my heart to call me out. I am a very loyal person and had it not been for such a heartbreaking incident I would have stayed just because of my guilt of leaving my family behind. However, when they did not seem to care about me, I decided I had enough. When the spelling bee incident happened it was the first time in my twelve years of life that I could not create an excuse for their behavior.

I have a sensitive heart that never wanted to see the truth about my abusers. I wanted to believe that it was my fault because then I could believe they were good people and I was so bad they had to hurt me. The spelling bee incident shattered this belief. I could not come up with anything I had done wrong. This time I saw them clearly for who they were and I could no longer believe otherwise. They pretended to be dedicated to the church, but their actions revealed they were only dedicated to their own reputation.

Time gives us a new perspective. I can tell when I'm living in the flesh and not the Spirit by the questions I ask. When I'm living in the flesh, during hard times, I ask, "Lord, why me, what are you doing to me?" When I'm living in the Spirit, during hard times I ask Lord, "What do you want me to know, what are you trying to show me about me? What area of my life are you trying to grow in me? What do you want to change in me?" The Spirit perspective knows that God wants what is best and if he allows any circumstance he will turn it around for our best no matter how impossible the idea seems.

Most of us miss these opportunities (pain and suffering) because we can't see past the pain of the circumstance to ask the Lord what HE might be doing. We can look around and see clearly what the devil is doing, but what is the Lord doing? We do believe he is still at work, don't we?

We must remember that God bought us with a high price

and we no longer belong to ourselves; this is his life we are living. If we demand our own way we have lost sight of the fact that this is his life we are living. We don't have a right to say no to the circumstances we find ourselves in. We must surrender and ask for wisdom on how to handle our stressful circumstances.

The problem is we think we know what is best for us. We don't. The Lord's protection is always to protect us from our "self." If we have to have what we want every day we will be miserable wretches and go to the grave miserable.

If we are here to do God's purposes and we allow him to direct and submit to his path for our lives, then we will be content no matter what the circumstances may be.

We trust that God knows what he is doing even if it makes no sense to us. When we are submitted to the Lord's will we can be confident that he has gone before us and is making a way for us to be free from ourselves.

True freedom is being in slavery to the Holy Spirit. When we want what we want we are in slavery to our flesh and it's a prison like none other.

Chapter Six
The Rebellion

L et's continue with what happened when I ran away that night after the spelling bee incident. I had gone to my friend's house and I cut my hair to shoulder length and received bangs. My hair had been down to my rear end where I could sit on it at times. The Amish stood for not cutting women's hair, so I rebelled and cut it off as a way of making a statement.

I was enjoying myself at my friend's house until she mentioned that I would never see my niece again if I didn't return home. I did love my niece very much and the thought of never seeing her was the only reason to return home. We had taken the phones off the hook so that my parents could not call and find me. I knew they had found my note that said they had a made a big mistake and I was not coming back. I knew they would try to call my friend's house.

The phone rang and we all jumped. "Who put the phone on the hook again?"

My friend's nephew had used the phone and placed it back on the hook. My friend's mom told me she would not lie for me. She answered the phone and handed the phone to me. "It's your mother."

I had many thoughts race through my mind. I did not want to return home. Yet, I did want to see my niece. After a long pause, I reluctantly answered the phone and spoke with my mother. I was cold and angry and Mom was crying; that is all I remember about the conversation, besides thinking I had to go home because of my niece.

I went home in body, but not in spirit or heart. My heart was broken and my spirit crushed. My parents had crossed a line and from that day forward I told them where I would go and what I would do and they did not try to stop me. I believe it was because they were afraid that I would run away again and make them look bad to the Amish community.

After I returned home I could not go to church because I could not get my hair to stay under my covering and so I stayed at home until my hair grew out enough to be put under a covering. Prior to running away I was a soft sensitive person. After I ran away I came back a very angry rebellious teenager. I walked with purpose and confidence and no one was going to get to me anymore. No one was going to control me or tell me what to do. **I became my own God.**

The teachers in school commented on my attitude change in eighth grade and my grades dropped. I could no longer concentrate. I had been a straight-A student, but after the incident I received a couple of B's. I had an "I don't care attitude" towards any authority figure. I felt at this point that authority figures where only there to rob me of life, not to protect me.

I was not allowed to continue beyond an eighth grade education due to the Amish beliefs and their desire to keep everyone in the community. I didn't feel I was anybody to anyone and as soon as I could I was going to go out there and be somebody.

During the eighth grade I went through puberty and I gained ten pounds and developed breasts. I did not gain any fat, just breasts. Since I was well endowed, even in my Amish dress it was noticeable and to my complete disgust, I started getting stares from many men. I could feel them undressing me with their eyes. The worst man was my dad. He started to stare at my breasts and I felt disgusting, shameful and like a whore. I felt like screaming at anyone who was staring at my chest while they were talking to me. Little did I know that I had been sexually molested at an early age. I had completely dissociated the abuse, but when men would look at me, especially my dad, I felt dirty through and through.

These lustful looks were triggering the deep-down dirtiness I already felt from prior abuse. Of course there is no way to prove that my dad and these other men were thinking lustful thoughts when they looked at me. However, I felt that deep-down, dirty feeling and wanted to slap each man who stared at me. These feelings are subjective and hard to explain in words. I wanted to cover up my breasts and wear a gunny sack. I developed bad posture as a result of feeling shame about my breasts. I hunched over in hopes they could not see them as well. I felt shame when my dad and other men looked at my breasts.

Logically I wonder, why is it that I should have felt shame for being well endowed? Shouldn't the one who is lusting be the one who feels the shame? Somehow this shame of what others did to me followed me through to adulthood. I took on my perpetrator's shame.

Soon after eighth grade, my cousin was due to have her fifth child. I was asked to be her nanny a week before the birth and for six weeks after the birth. My cousin and her husband lived as most of the Amish did, without electricity or phone. I should have been used to lighting kerosene lamps and not having a phone; however, due to our special situation I did not have these skills.

It proved to be a brand new experience for me in my teenage years. My cousin also did not have running water to their woodshed where the laundry was done twice a week. Most mornings I would get up at five a.m. and prepare lunches for the husband to take to work and the children to take to school. I would then make breakfast for three adults and four children. Boxed cereal was not a luxury for this family. Breakfast was made from scratch with eggs that came from their own chickens and hash-browns shredded by hand from potatoes grown in the garden. At times I would make oatmeal or French toast.

On the mornings when I had to do laundry, in spite of it being the dead of winter and bitterly cold, I went to the wood shed and built a fire under a big iron bowl. It was called the water kettle. I would hand pump water into a gutter that would allow the water to run into the kettle and then I would build a fire under the kettle and heat the water. I used this water to do the laundry by hand through an old time washing machine. We hung laundry out on the clothesline even if it freeze dried. It was a challenge to bring the stiff boards of clothing into the house afterward. The dresses were especially difficult to get through the doorways into the house. The arms would freeze and the dresses would look like a stick person. Trying to maneuver them through the doorways was humorous.

I learned how to work hard and do the duties of a housewife and mother of five children. I cleaned the house and I got up in the middle of the night when the children vomited.

The family invited me into their family and I became a mother to all the children and the joy of being part of their family was greater than the work I had to do. After about three weeks of working for my cousin, my sister thought it would be nice if I went home for a couple of days to see Mom and Dad. I thought I might actually be glad to see Dad after three weeks and maybe he would be glad, too.

As soon as we stepped foot in the house, Dad did not even say "hi" to me. He started yelling at my sister for staying the night with her horse. The problem was her horse was going to be in his barn for the night and would be eating his hay. I was shocked and I told my sister I wanted to go back to my cousin's the next day. I could not believe that after three weeks my dad was so focused on money that he could not even be glad to see me.

My cousin was glad to see me back and I told them I wanted to stay with them as long as I could. They understood and were sad that my dad had reacted the way he did. My cousin's husband did not yell and cause tension in the home; it was a relaxed, loving environment. If my family had been as nice as my cousin's family I might still be living the Amish lifestyle. However, I could not live the Amish lifestyle under the same roof as my dad. There are a lot of great Amish families out there; I didn't get the luxury of being raised in one.

Many people who have heard my story have questioned the Amish faith and their way of living. ***Let me make it perfectly clear that there are many good Christian Amish people whom I still love dearly.*** Amish people are human just like everyone reading this book. The percentage of abuse/neglect in the Amish is in direct proportion to the fact that they are human as well as all those who are reading this book. Choosing an isolated way of life will not protect anyone from the natural sin nature that is available within all of us. It's a choice to live from our sin nature or to be born again and live from our spirit nature. A life lived from our sin nature produces lying, cheating, adultery, jealousy, and death (Galatians 5:19-21). ***A life lived from the spirit, the Holy Spirit, is joy, peace, patience, kindness and self-control (Galatians 5:22-23).***

The Amish lifestyle is a choice to live separate from the world, and many of them believe Christ died for their sins and they need him to save them from their sins. They believe that the things of the world such as cars, electricity, modern technology, the media, and politics all get in the way of serving our Lord.

I have to say I think they are right. TV, computers and social media can get in the way of serving our Lord. However, I also happen to believe that these same tools can be used in a positive way and we can serve the Lord by balancing our time. We can choose to turn off all technology and spend time in silence and meditation with our Lord.

So, I don't advise for or against living the Amish lifestyle. I am for our Lord Jesus Christ and living for him. I had a bad experience in my childhood because of evil in our home and I just happened to be Amish, as well.

Chapter Seven
Adventure

There is a time in the life of an Amish teenager that most people know about from books and TV shows called "Rummspringa." Translated, it means "running around." If there is one thing I will never understand about the Amish, it's why they shelter their children from everything until they are sixteen and then let them go out and experience the world. This is like turning loose an untamed animal with no skill and no self-control. It's a disaster waiting to happen. It's the time when teenagers are allowed to date and be gone for the weekend and they drink and have sex and whatever else they can get their hands on to do.

Some Amish parents have been enlightened and are letting their children go little by little, and are setting boundaries. However, this was not my experience. For me, there were no boundaries in our home. Dad was allowed to scream and yell and threaten to kill people and burn their houses down and hope they were in it. I had learned that I had no right to my own body. So it's no wonder I acted out with rebellion fighting for my own rights to think what I wanted to think, to feel what I wanted to feel and to do what I wanted to do.

One Sunday morning while my parents were at church, I decided to take my dad's work car out of the garage and drive it. For a sixteen-year-old Amish girl this was the most exciting thing available to me at the time. This old green boat of a car was so old that it only had AM radio. I didn't care. I found some shorts and a tee shirt of Caleb's, and I put my hair up in a ponytail and I went out for a joy ride. Oh, but not without others to enjoy this with me. Forbidden fruit is never good alone. I drove to the neighbor's and picked up a fifteen-year-old boy, a thirteen-year-old girl, and a young, eight-year-old girl. Their dad was actually at the hospital picking up their mom after a surgery.

We were all on cloud nine. This was wrong in so many ways and so the rush was like what one might experience robbing a bank. We were being criminals in a lot of different ways, according to the Amish. The only law we were breaking according to state law was the fact that I was driving without a license. To break the Amish law was more rebellious than to break the state law. We had no idea what it meant to break the state law and get in trouble, but we knew what it meant to break the Amish law and get in trouble. It was an adrenaline rush for us all.

We drove around in the country, and just so we could be a little bit more rebellious, we drove right by the Amish house where my mom and dad were at church. The fact that we could do this made it so much more exciting and wrong. We decided to drive to a gas station and buy some cigarettes. This would make us just a little more rebellious towards everything we were taught not to do. At times I would find myself traveling at about seventy miles an hour, windows down, smoking cigarettes. We were living the dangerous adventurous life. I could drive about fifteen miles an hour with the horse and buggy and about twenty with my bicycle, so seventy was pretty fast.

The last mile before we reached home I decided to let the fifteen-year-old boy drive. We were driving at a rate of eighty miles an hour, and then the young teenager started pumping the brake and shouting, "It's not stopping!!"

My heart stopped. We were fast approaching an intersection. At this point I was sitting in the front middle seat with the thirteen-year-old girl to my right. The thirteen-year-old was freaking out and reached for the door saying she was going to jump out. I grabbed her arm and in my best commanding voice I ordered her to stay seated. I continued to shout that we were driving eighty miles an hour and she would not survive if she jumped out. I reached over towards the driver and turned the key. I figured eventually we would stop if the engine was off.

I then proceeded to grab the gear shift and put it in reverse for a second while the car jerked and squealed and slowed down. Then I put it back in drive, and then back in reverse, until the car came to a stop. We went through the intersection at probably forty-five miles an hour. Thank goodness no one was coming because we could not have stopped. We were so shaken that we got out and pushed the car back home, which was about a half mile. I could have started the engine again, but I was so scared I didn't want to do anything but get the car back in the garage before anyone saw us.

The car was very long and wide. Even if we had the engine running it would have been hard to put it back in its exact spot on the dirt floor garage where my dad kept it. So to push it forward and back and forward and back until it was on the right dirt hole where he kept the back tires was a very hard job.

The thrill we had felt at the beginning of our adventure was replaced with sheer terror. I had to make sure the car was back in the right spot, and make sure the kids went home and didn't tell their parents. I had to get the smoke smell off of me and get rid of my clothes before my parents came home.

After the car was in place, keys back in their place, and

the kids gone home, I sat down and stared into space, took a deep breath, and said out loud, "There must be a God!" We could all have died had the brakes stopped working on our approach to the busy highway where we went to get our cigarettes. If they had stopped working when we were traveling around the sharp curves miles from home we could have ended up in the field. My dad would have been so mad and we would have gotten in trouble with his boss, the one who owned the car.

Wow, we escaped by the hair of our chins. I knew I did not deserve to be saved from the tragedy that could have taken place. I had never felt protected by my family, but in this moment I felt there must a greater being out there who had watched out for me that day. What if I would have killed my three neighbor friends? What if I had pulled out in front of someone on the busy highway and killed others and us?

Looking back on that experience I think the Lord taught me a better lesson than my parents ever could have. I felt this unspeakable presence had protected me that day when I thought I was having fun. Imagine how that day could have changed my life forever. The experience did change it, but in a good way.

I could have been paralyzed that day and stuck in the Amish lifestyle the rest of my life. My life would have taken a different turn. I shiver now as an adult looking back. I praise Jesus for his protection when I was completely rebellious. That was undeserved grace.

Chapter Eight
On My Own

At the ripe old age of seventeen, on New Year's Eve, I started the New Year out right when I moved out of my parents' home. I was so very relieved. The New Year was 1992 and I moved into an apartment with another Amish girl who was looking for a roommate. I did not know her and she did not know me. But she had heard that I was looking to move into town. This was a small town, just 2,500 in population, but I had lived in the country for seventeen years, so this was exciting.

I remember that first night like it was yesterday. I opened the refrigerator door real wide and just stood there. No one was yelling at me and telling me to close the refrigerator door. I left the lights on in my room all night.

All these things my dad would yell about because he did not want us to use too much electricity. I remember lying in my bed and saying to myself, "Wow, listen to the silence. No one is yelling." I remember smiling and falling into a deep comfortable safe sleep.

For the first time in my seventeen years of life I felt safe. *This brings tears to my eyes as I write this, how awful that I had to leave my family at age seventeen in order to feel safe.* This is not an exaggerated statement, for even when my dad was gone for the day I knew he was coming back and I never felt I could relax and drop my guard. I was on duty all the time, as I would imagine a soldier during a time of combat.

Many people ask me how I made it on my own. "You must have had so much courage to step out on your own," they say. I look back and remember feeling so relieved to get out that I don't remember it taking any courage.

As I think about the environment of my parents' house I feel a cold, eerie feeling that makes my skin crawl. Most jails probably had a warmer environment than my parents' home. The walls had wallpaper that was falling off, exposing the drywall underneath which was also chipping. The ceilings of the old house were taped in spots to keep the drywall from falling on us. The house did not look like this because we were poor. It was because Dad refused to spend money on a house that was not ours.

The house was hideous inside and out, but the worst part was the presence in the home. During the day when Dad was at work there was a sad, lifeless silence. When he came home there was an unexplainable anger that filled the air. It was what I imagine one would feel in a concentration camp. You didn't know when the enemy would attack and from which angle. Would it be with words or with physical attacks or the throwing of objects? Mom just hung her head and stayed in the room no matter how bad the battle got. She had died inside and was numb in order to handle the battlefield.

The reason I knew I had to leave at seventeen was because I was no longer able to eat at the same table with my dad. My hatred for him had taken over my body. I could not digest food in his presence. I knew I must get out for my own sake or I would soon become like him.

Little did I know I had already become an angry person like my dad.

My sister Maria was very upset that I left Mom there alone with the beast. I told Maria I was going to move out and take care of myself. She thought that was selfish. I did not think that I was helping my parents' situation because I would get angry at Dad when he got angry. Mom was just quiet and did not add fuel to the fire. I, on the other hand, would speak up and let him have it. At this point Maria and Jonathan were both married and gone from the home, and Caleb had moved out. I knew it was time for me to go as well.

My relationship with some members of my family felt very controlling and I did not know why. I had blocked the memories of sexual abuse. It was not until I fell in love that the memory of the abuse came flooding back.

My family, except for Caleb, did not speak a word to me for a year after I moved out. Caleb lived in the same little town and owned a video and arcade where I worked on weekends. I would work forty-five to fifty hours per week at a woodworking business, Monday through Friday and some Saturdays. I sanded kitchen cabinet doors and prepared them to be stained and sprayed. I was known to be one of the fastest and best sanders. I was often offered extra hours to work early and/or late. My dad had told me I would not make it out on my own because I was going to spend too much money on electricity. I laugh at that thought now.

Either way I set out to prove him wrong, and prove him wrong I did. I took every opportunity to work overtime at my full time job and then worked until one a.m. on Saturday nights at the arcade. I worked seven days a week and slept in on Sunday mornings.

I enrolled in a GED class and graduated the same year as my regular high school graduating class.

I met Patrick at the arcade. He would come in and stand around the counter making flirtatious comments towards me. I tried not to seem too eager, but I was shocked that he would want anything to do with me. My insides would flip flop when I would hear the door jingle and look up to see it was him. I would pretend I was as cool as a cucumber and that I was busy with other customers. Inside I was acting like a little school girl waiting for her prom date to ask her out.

Patrick was popular in the Amish community and so I was surprised when one day he asked me out. I was exhilarated. We had a lot of fun together. We talked until the wee hours of the night and laughed until our sides hurt. We were soul mates. He would open my doors for me. I was smitten. No one had ever been this nice to me. I was not popular in the Amish community, so I was shocked that he wanted me. *I felt like the star quarterback picks the plain ugly girl in school. I truly felt special and head over heels in love like never before.*

Prior to this relationship, I had a few other relationships that turned sour. But I felt this man was my Prince Charming. He was too good to be true and I could not figure out what he wanted with me; however, I embraced the relationship with joy.

I did not know what to do with the memory of sexual abuse. In fact, I was oblivious to the fact that it was abuse. The memory was so removed from me it was like I was watching a movie of someone else; when the memory came to my mind, I basically pushed it under the rug because I could. I did not feel any emotional connection to the memory and I sure didn't want to tell anyone that I had been sexually active as a young child. This was embarrassing and shameful to me. I ignored the memory and kept working and never said a word.

At the time I met Patrick I did not know the Lord. I wanted nothing to do with church, but Patrick wanted me to go to church with him. Reluctantly I went with him to a Mennonite Church.

Right away, after the first service, I told Patrick that there was too much love there and they must want something from me. I let him know I would not be going back. At this time in my life every other word out of my mouth was a swear word.

He would ask me to please stop, that it hurt his heart. I would roll my eyes and try to control my tongue.

Two weeks after I met Patrick, I was offered a job to be a nanny for professional football player. My heart sunk. I knew that Patrick would not want me to leave. We had already bonded on a deep level and I knew how he would feel about it. I asked him anyway and got the answer I thought I would get, which was, of course, "I don't want you to move three hours away."

I look back at this experience and see God's protection. Had I not been dating Patrick I would have taken that opportunity to get out of the small town and leave my Amish life completely behind. However, I had not met the Lord yet and I cannot imagine what would have happened had I moved to a big city at that age.

Even when I did not know the Lord, he was there protecting me. The same is true with my experience of running away. My friend reminded me that I would not ever see my niece again, so I returned home instead of living out on the streets and not finishing eighth grade. Both of these events would have been life-changing had the Lord allowed them to happen. How could I forget the car ride when the brakes stopped working? It could have changed my life if the outcome had been different.

Another area in which the Lord protected me was he allowed me to find the joy of running. At the age of twelve, while still living at home with my parents, I heard about endorphins and I thought it was the neatest thing ever, so I started running around the country section, four miles a day. Life was hard and I hated to return home, but it was more tolerable after that daily four-mile run.

I use to run in my Amish dress and I would sneak a little radio with headphones and put them on after I was away from the house. I would listen to 94.5 FM, a soft rock station where I would hear songs like, "Right Here Waiting For You," by Richard Marx. I would dream about that man who would sit with me and hold my hand and kiss me gently.

I learned to run and get the **natural drug of endorphins instead of getting hooked on street drugs**, which could have happened, but by God's grace, did not. Only by God's grace!

Chapter Nine
The Change Begins

I was working for a woodworking company sanding doors at the time I met Patrick. About six months after we started dating, Patrick's parents asked me to work for them as an office manager. They also owned an Amish woodworking business, so Patrick, who worked in the hardware department, and I both worked for his parents.

Patrick would assemble the finished product. As one can imagine there were a few hurdles to jump over working for your boyfriend's parents, after dating only six months. As a couple, Patrick and I jumped those hurdles, along with his parents, and considering my history, I thought it went well.

Our boss, Patrick's dad, asked us and some other colleagues to take the Dale Carnegie course on human relationships. The purpose of sending us to take the Dale Carnegie course was to build positive relationships among the workers. I had no idea how the Dale Carnegie course would affect me.

John was Patrick's graduate assistant and would call him weekly to see if he needed help with his assignments. The graduate assistant was someone who had taken the Dale Carnegie course and volunteered his time to help future classmates through the twelve-week program. John offered to take us out to dinner one weekend.

John and his wife Frieda had also grown up Amish and were now a part of the Amish Mennonite Church. We were shocked that this young godly couple had any interest in us.

After they took us out to dinner they started asking me questions about what I thought of God. I said, "God?" The thought of God really never entered my mind because he seemed to me to be a foreign, standoffish kind of person. I thought if he was Amish I sure wanted nothing to do with him. I had been told that if I was not going to be Amish I would go to hell. I decided if I was hell bent I might as well do it right and have fun. I was an all or nothing person. So, prior to this conversation with John and Frieda, I had no interest in this Amish God, as I knew him.

That night John and Frieda told me that *I did not have to be Amish to be a Christian.* I was shocked. No one had ever bothered to share this information with me. I shared with them about how much I hated my dad and how I did not want anything to do with an Amish God. They gently shared that God is a forgiving God and that I needed to accept Christ as my Savior in order to be saved. They asked me if I wanted to accept Christ. I was very hesitant and responded to them like one would respond to a door-to-door salesman.

I wasn't sure what they were selling and I was leery about what it meant to accept Jesus. It didn't make any sense to me and so I shared that I didn't want to just do something because they told me to, I wanted it to mean something to me and at this point accepting Jesus would not mean anything to me.

At the end of the night we pulled into their driveway and were sitting in their minivan talking and they asked me if they could pray for me. I was very uncomfortable and felt embarrassed, but I reluctantly said okay, because I didn't want to offend them. They had taken an interest in us and I felt honored that they wanted to spend time with us and seemed to be interested in what was best for us. Through the years no one had bothered to take interest in me, so I wanted to listen.

I have no idea what they prayed that night in the minivan in front of their little house, but I felt hot from the top of my head to the tips of my toes. Before we bowed our head I had simply thought in my heart that, well, if God wasn't Amish, I would consider hearing more about him. If I did not have to be Amish to be a Christian and join him in heaven someday I would be open to it.

It's very important to note that I did not accept Christ that night. I did not even speak out loud saying that I might be interested in a God who was not Amish. As far as John and Frieda were concerned, I did not make any verbal progression towards the Lord. However, the Lord heard my heart; *all I did was tilt my heart towards the possibility and the Lord took that as an opportunity to reach me. He started pursuing me.*

Patrick and I went home to our separate apartments and I felt so soft and beautiful the next day. I had a horrible ugly habit of swearing with every other sentence that I spoke. After that prayer I immediately stopped swearing. I couldn't do it. It was the most amazing thing that had happened to me so far. I was still cautious and skeptical about this Jesus person, but I felt warm and soft.

Looking back, I realize God heard me that day. **All he needed was for me to say in my heart that I was open to a God who was not Amish.** I believe the Holy Spirit came upon me that day and I stopped swearing. I loved how I felt. This was my first experience with the living God.

At the end of the Dale Carnegie course, to my boss's dismay, I chose to change careers, return to school and wanted to eventually go to church. Within a couple of months I changed careers to serving tables at a local Amish-style restaurant. I loved the interaction with my customers and I was very good at serving and received many compliments. I was not used to receiving compliments, but it felt good.

I enrolled at a local community college with a major in psychology. I wanted to be a counselor because I was always intrigued and wanted to understand why humans did what they did, especially myself and my family.

Patrick and I dated for three years. In the second year I started to notice that Patrick was drinking more and was swearing, as well. I did not like how Patrick was changing.

I had a fear that the man I might marry would become an alcoholic and abuse our children. One night Patrick came to my apartment after a softball game and I could smell the alcohol on his breath. He appeared intoxicated and was curt with me and did not want to talk as we normally did.

Our custom was that he would come to my apartment and we would share the events of our day and then he would go home to his apartment. He didn't stay very long, and excused himself to go home to his apartment, which was only four blocks away.

I laid there for about three hours, unable to sleep, with visions of marrying a mean alcoholic and having him abuse our children. I got scared and I rode my bike to his apartment at two a.m. I was sobbing and begged him, please, to go back to church. He woke up and sat bolt upright in bed and said, "Okay, let's go to church."

That Sunday we went to the Mennonite Church and continued to attend church thereafter. The following Sunday we went to the Mennonite Church where Patrick had been attending before he met me. I was still somewhat uncomfortable, but I wanted my old Patrick back and so I knew this was what we needed to do.

Soon after we starting attending church in 1994, I accepted Christ as my Savior and my heart and spirit started to soften. It had been six months to a year since my experience with John and Frieda and now I took the next step to actually invite Jesus into my heart as my Lord and Savior. Once again I felt hot from the top of my head to the tips of my toes and I am sure my cheeks were flushed for days. I had taken *another step towards my loving Jesus.*

As we were going through a membership course we were told that baptism was part of becoming a Christian. The Mennonite Church's custom was to sprinkle a member to represent baptism. I didn't understand it, but wanted to do whatever I was supposed to do in order to be a Christian. One thing I knew was that I liked who Patrick was when I met him and I didn't like who he was becoming since he had not been attending church.

I did not fully understand what it meant to accept Christ as my Savior, but I knew I was ready to take that next step. However, there was not much life change for me. I simply went to church and before I had not been attending church. I was simply a church goer. I did not pray or read my Bible.

Thanks to my dad for suggesting I could not make it on my own, I had saved enough money to put down on a house when Patrick and I were married. The house cost $31,000 and it was the size of a two-car garage, but it was a great starter house. I thought things were okay between Patrick and me, until about three months into our marriage when *something seemed to be standing in between us.* I felt disconnected from Patrick and blamed myself because of my past with my father. I thought I must be expecting too much.

I wondered if this feeling I had towards Patrick was connected to my hurtful childhood. At times I would feel I was a child again and it would scare me. I never wanted to go back there. I really wanted to forget my childhood ever happened. What I could consciously remember from my childhood was that I never felt safe or loved, and always felt like the butt of jokes. I hoped that would all stay in my past and I could start a new life with Patrick.

About a year after Patrick and I were married, a summer tent revival came to town on the same night Patrick's softball game was scheduled. Patrick's brother and sister-in-law were going with us. One of us had to run back in to get a drink and the phone rang. Softball was canceled. We all looked at each other and decided we should go to the revival instead. So we changed out of our shorts and went to church.

That night the evangelist spoke about someone he had encountered in his travels who was bitter towards a father. The evangelist repeated, "I hate my dad, I hate my dad!"

I felt my heart stand still and tears well up in my eyes and stream down my face. This was a miracle. One thing you must know is that in the past I could not cry. In times prior to this night I would feel pain but I would not be able to cry as there was a disconnect between my brain and my heart.

An example of this was when my friend had a miscarriage and I said very bluntly, "Well, you can have more." It was very hurtful to her, but I did not mean it in a hurtful way, I just could not feel, so I said things that were hurtful.

That night after the evangelist preached and the altar call was announced, I ran to the altar. I knew God was calling my name. I shared with those at the altar that I thought I had forgiven my dad, but I guessed I hadn't. They asked me if I would pray to forgive him and I said, "I don't think I can," and I started to give all the reasons why I couldn't.

After much conversation about why I couldn't forgive my dad, the pastor called over one of the lay counselors who traveled with the tent revival. The counselor shared some lame story of why he had a hard time forgiving his dad. I felt it did not compare to what I had to forgive. I did not like his spirit and attitude, but I smiled and nodded and pretended I was interested. Finally he said, "Will you pray to forgive your father?" I reluctantly said I would pray and say the words, but I didn't think it was possible to forgive.

A miracle happened as the counselor laid his hand on my shoulder and prayed. I felt lifted up out of my chair and as if I was Forest Gump with braces all over my body. It all fell off of me and my eyes were opened and I could see. As I opened my eyes after the prayer, *I felt all the bitterness towards my father had gone!* I felt like a new person! This was a life-changing event.

The problem with this change started the next day when *I begin to cry and could not stop.* Prior to this I could not cry at all and now the faucet would not turn off.

I was an adult but *felt like a little five-year-old girl and I wanted a daddy to hold me.* This was the strangest thing I had ever experienced. I kept asking to meet with the lay counselor and I told him that I had this desire for him to hold me as a father, and I didn't know what to do. I knew I was an adult, but felt five and was jealous when I saw him hold his children. I met with him and his wife and I begged them to help me. I was so embarrassed, and to make matters worse, the counselor announced at the prayer meeting that I wanted him to hold me. Of course in a town of 2,500 people everyone talks, so it wasn't long before my reputation became that of a sort of whore.

Obviously this was not my heart's motive. This was the first time my heart had been open since it was shut down by my family. I trusted my new church family and once again I was misunderstood and made out to be someone I was not. The feeling was similar to what I had felt as a child in my home. Hope deferred makes the heart sick and my heart was sick because I had hoped my relationships would be different with my new church family.

Patrick did not like when I was crying. There were a couple of times I had to come home from work in the middle of the day because I had fallen apart. He was upset and told me to grow up. **No one in my life knew what to do with**

this pain that was coming out of me, including me. Like driving in heavy fog, I felt lost and alone.

I was so desperate for someone, anyone, to help me that I even stayed in touch with the lay counselor after he left town. After a month, the lay counselor told me that I was a hard person to counsel and that he felt sorry for my poor husband and that he never wanted to see me again. This shut my heart down and I stopped crying.

I was somewhat relieved because I no longer felt that need for a daddy. I felt my heart had been misunderstood and shamed again after I had opened my heart and its raw emotions to the wrong people. Since I know the rest of the story I know that this happened too many times on my road to healing. I was hurt many more times in the same ways I had been abused and neglected as a child.

I had been taking classes at a community college, working towards my associate degree in Psychology, but during the revival when I fell apart I canceled my fall classes and registered for a six-week semester at a Bible college. I also started Bible Study Fellowship, which is an eight-year Bible study that is in-depth enough to be a college course. After the revival and the breaking open of the shell of my heart, I had a hunger for God's Word like I never had before.

While I was attending the Bible college, I immersed myself in God's Word and I loved it. I spent every day in the Word and researching the Word. I was on cloud nine.

Patrick came to visit me after I had been there for two weeks and since we were married we were allowed to stay in one of the apartments for the weekend. I stayed in the dorm with the girls the rest of the six-week term.

After the six weeks at the Bible college I returned home and was trying to decide if I would go back to school or what would be my next step. I had not had my period for two months and I thought there was very little chance I was pregnant, but would check it anyway. Patrick had visited one weekend and it was the weekend that I was supposed to be menstruating, so of course I thought there was no possibility of being pregnant. We had not planned to have a child yet and so we would watch the calendar and used protection during the times I should be ovulating. The plan worked for a year and a half. I thought I had skipped my period the first month because I was in a different environment and my body was just messed up.

I bought the pregnancy test and learned almost within two seconds I was pregnant! I was so excited; I could not retain my joy. I jumped up and down and shouted, "I'm going to have a baby! I'm going to have a baby!" I had not told Patrick because he was at work, but I had to tell someone so I called the restaurant where I worked and I told some of my friends there. Patrick's aunt worked there and I shouted it to her. I kept repeating, "I'm going to have a baby." You'd thought I'd won the lottery. I recall the commercials of the guy showing up at someone's door telling the person he had won the lottery and he would go crazy, jumping up and down and possibly falling down. *That was how I felt. I had won the lottery; I was going to have my own baby.*

That night when Patrick arrived home I told him to sit on the couch. I shouted, "We're going to have a baby," and he seemed stunned. It took him a bit to understand what I was saying.

I absolutely loved being pregnant. I never felt alone. I had an uncomplicated pregnancy and an uncomplicated delivery and I still love my little precious bundle. He is now all grown up, about six feet tall, and has a driver's license, but he will always be my precious bundle in my heart. I used to have "Precious" as his contact name, but he removed it from my phone and replaced it with his name.

I remember that day when we brought him home. I asked

Patrick to drive real slowly because I didn't want to jostle my little guy in his car seat. We brought him into our six-hundred and seventy square-foot house and I sat in the rocker and I looked down at this little helpless redheaded child and I began to cry. *How could I be responsible for a life? I hardly knew how to handle my own life.*

The only parenting information I had in my mind was from my parents and that information needed to be deleted as far as I was concerned. I had a friend, Sherry, who I would call daily and she would answer my questions about parenting.

Sherry had taken some parenting classes and so she shared her insights with me. I was supposed to let my baby cry to sleep instead of rocking him. It broke my heart to hear him cry. Just when I was about to give up that he would learn to put himself to sleep, he got it and started to go to sleep on his own. Later, I did understand how it helped my son become more independent.

I took advice, of course, from Sherry because she had four children of her own, but I also added my own unique style to parenting. I would talk to my son as if he was an adult, even when he was only six months old. I taught him sign language so he could ask for a drink or get more, or say "all done." I always talked to him about Jesus and how we could do nothing on our own. At times when I was in pain, I would pray and ask the Lord to please protect my son from my emotions and pain. There were many times in my son's childhood that I did not feel capable of being a mother, but I prayed hard and gave it all I had.

Needless to say, we made it through his growing up years. He has turned out to be a fine young gentleman. We must have done okay in spite of all the insecurities and pain in my life. **God is good; it wasn't our parenting, but God is simply good, no ifs, ands, or buts about it.**

Chapter Ten
Not Again

The next time I felt like a five-year-old was two years after the tent meeting, when I had a one-year-old child of my own. At that time, I met a compassionate, merciful man who was selling a healthcare product that would help my tendonitis. I was working at an Amish-style restaurant as a server and wore a brace on my wrist. This man asked me if he could help me with my wrist and we started talking. My husband and I signed up with his network marketing company and we started to spend a lot of time with him.

After about two months of spending time with this man I started to feel overwhelmed by these being-a-five-year-old, needing-a-daddy emotions. They were strong and powerful and drove me to get the need met. I explained this to the man and his wife. I was embarrassed, but they did not shame me. However, it was a difficult situation and I soon realized that my need for him to be my daddy was not going to lead to anything healthy and I ended our relationship.

We had not stayed in contact with John and Frieda, but they lived in the same little town and found out that I was struggling with the problem of feeling like a little girl. They called me one day and shared about a counseling center that understood those kinds of issues and gave me the center's contact information.

At the counseling center I was diagnosed with Dissociate Identity Disorder. Basically this happens when a person survives abuse/trauma and is able to separate the abuse into different files into the left hemisphere of the brain.

I was intrigued because they had an explanation for what I was going through. My trigger seemed to be men who either looked like my dad when he was young, or who had merciful daddy hearts.

This disorder, as I understood it, was a defense mechanism. When, as a young child, I could not handle the trauma and abuse, I would separate it in the library of my mind and go on as if nothing had happened to me. I created new personalities or parts to handle life. I understood that if I had not been able to separate the traumatic events I would not have coped or survived in society.

This explained why I could not cry before the Lord softened my heart. The hard part about discovering feeling in my heart was that the pain was so intense I needed help to get through it. It was a doubled-edged sword. I wanted to be healed, but in order to heal I had to go through pain that I did not want to experience, and it made me very vulnerable.

Like an onion, I had many layers. I started driving three hours to this counseling center where I met with a Christian counselor whom I shall name Todd. I would stay at a nearby hotel and my sessions were three hours long for five days. Todd and I started working through my layers and I was just as surprised as he was because I didn't know what was inside my heart and was shocked as we started to uncover memories.

During this time my marriage to Patrick was unraveling. I asked my husband if he had committed adultery and he said no. I decided the problem was me and I needed to get help. I assumed my lack of respect for Patrick was because of my need for healing.

My husband let me go to counseling thinking our problems were entirely my fault. The closer I got to the Lord, the further I seemed to get from my husband. I could not figure out what was happening. I would spend hours alone with the Lord, journaling and begging him to tell me the truth about my past and also to give me a love for my husband.

My husband would get upset with me because I would spend so much time alone with the Lord and he would make statements such as, "Well, not everyone has to spend three hours with the Lord every day." This is the same husband who wanted me to go to church with him and stop swearing when I met him. Something had changed.

During this time I was also crying out to God about the prayer covering that the Mennonite Church believed women should wear on their heads. I was not convicted to wear the prayer covering. I felt I was just doing it to look good to the church and so I stopped wearing it. Of course I received a lot of questions on why I stopped. My husband and I then decided to stop going to the Mennonite Church and we started attending a non-denominational Christian church.

My son was about two years old when I started counseling and it became very hard to be a mother when I was feeling like a five-year-old, crying, broken child. I prayed hard that my son would not feel what I was going through. I wanted to stop the cycle of abuse/neglect with my generation.

I claimed the Lord's promises to be close to the brokenhearted and answer my prayers for my son's protection and also for his future wife. I desperately wanted and still want a godly wife for my son.

My mother-in-law and my friend Sherry would help take care of my son while I worked or needed time alone with the Lord. I could not have done it without them to help me.

After about a year of counseling with Todd, he stopped being consistent in his responses to me. He would draw me close and then he would suddenly push me away, only in words, not physically. I was so fragile that I did not know what to do about Todd being real nice to me then cold and pushing me away. It made no sense to me. I was trying to put one foot in front of the other and carry out my duties as a wife and mother. I became more and more emotionally unstable as we peeled away the onion layers.

One night, while I was in the middle of one of my weeks of counseling with Todd, I visited the local bar to get away and get a drink. The next day, I shared with Todd that I was upset and had gone to the bar the night before and had a drink.

Todd was very angry with me and said I was making his counseling center look bad and they could not tolerate this kind of behavior. He brought in the director of the center, Dr. James.

I had seen Dr. James in the hallway at times and never felt comfortable. *Something didn't seem right about him and I didn't like him any more in person.* When he entered the counseling room he brought a big presence. He was over six feet tall, and had a very loud, commanding voice. I don't remember much of what was said that day. I only knew that I was told that if I ever went to a bar while I was there for counseling they would no longer counsel me. I felt ashamed.

After Dr. James left the room, I started crying because I knew I had disappointed Todd. Todd, however, had no compassion and said he had nothing left to say to me and that he could not help me until I stopped rebelling. I cried and cried as I felt completely helpless and hopeless.

Looking back at that experience I think what they did to intimidate me and shame me was very similar to how my abusive family treated me at home. I could not get out of the pain and even though I was still crying, Todd said I should go back to my hotel and think about what I had done. Todd's attitude and spirit was one of a disappointed parent punishing his child with the silent treatment. It was not that he couldn't help me; he chose to send me to my room, so to speak.

I came back to the center within an hour because I could not stop crying and I was scared. I was stuck in a memory and needed help to get through it. I begged Todd to help me but he had no compassion towards me and looked down his nose at me with contempt.

Todd exuded a spirit of punishment that was all too familiar to my broken soul. I was having a complete mental and emotional breakdown, but the one who would normally help me through this—Todd—wanted nothing to do with me.

They called my husband and asked him to drive the three hours to come be with me. It was an absolute disaster. I did not feel safe to share my heart with my husband and now I was no longer safe to share with Todd. I had made him angry and now he had rejected me just like my family. I felt like a trapped animal.

My husband arrived on a Thursday night and we had one more pre-planned three-hour session the next day with Todd. I was so fragile I did not know what to do. I didn't want to go, but I also didn't know where else I could go. So my husband and I went to see Todd.

Todd miraculously had a change of heart overnight. He was kind and spoke gently to me and said he was sorry that I was in so much pain and maybe we had a slight miscommunication the day before.

I was thinking, "Slight miscommunication!"?

I knew this was as close to an apology as I would get. It sounded like Todd had some time to cool down after his pride was injured from my visit to the bar. I don't remember the painful details of that counseling session, but I survived and drove three hours home.

Looking back now, the wisdom I would share with the reader is that if a counselor gets upset with you because you are making them look bad, then run away from this unhealthy counselor as fast as you can. If a counselor punishes you because of how you made them feel, RUN! A healthy counselor is consistent and does not change the way he treats his counselee based on the counselee's performance.

The sad reality is many counselors are unhealthy and are in the profession to satisfy a need within them to help others. This is revealed if the counselee does not perform as the counselor wants the client to perform. If the counselee changes and is successful then the counselor feels better, but if the client fails and gets worse after counseling with the counselor, the counselor may reject the client because they are not performing well, bringing the counselor's insecurities to the forefront.

Todd could not handle my emotional fragility and instead of admitting that to me in a kind way and helping me find someone else, he pushed me away by saying things that were hurtful.

Chapter Eleven
Betrayal

As Todd and I continued to remove layers of my heart, I was becoming more and more unstable emotionally. Around this same time, my husband and I had a hard conversation. I admitted that I didn't feel any love for him, but that I was praying and asking the Lord to help me feel love again. Divorce was not an option for either one of us so even though I was not having any feelings of love towards him, I still did not consider leaving him. We were taught that marriage was for a lifetime no matter what was going on in the marriage.

He immediately said we needed to see John and Frieda. He called them that night and we set up a time to go see them. They were now lay counselors taking couples through a marriage workbook to cleanse their marriages.

I don't recall how many sessions we had with them before it happened. One night I sensed that Patrick had some sexual immorality in his life and I was scared to know what it might be. Patrick got up and went to the bathroom and I said to John and Frieda, "I think he wrote something down about immorality in his workbook."

John said, "Tomorrow night's session is more about sexual immorality."

As Patrick came out of the bathroom John announced that if there were any sexual immorality issues we would cover that tomorrow night.

The next night Patrick said nothing to me about what he would share. We did our assignments on our own, and when we sat in front of John and Frieda, Patrick bowed his head and prayed for the Lord to forgive him for committing adultery with [blank and blank].

Even though I suspected some kind of immorality, I was shocked. I couldn't believe he had actually been with other women, especially since one of them was a very good friend of mine.

Patrick was not the type I'd suspect of adultery. He was quiet and appeared kind and sensitive. He had been with one of my best friends before our wedding and continued three months after we were married. He had withheld this information from me for five years. The feeling I had of someone standing in between us was real; it had been another woman.

I stared at John, looking for some help to handle this new information. John looked at me and said, "Your husband needs you right now."

"What? My husband needs ME?" My heart was like a shattered window already before this news, and when John said my husband needed me, I felt like someone took a sledgehammer and put a big hole in my heart. Within thirty minutes I had a migraine and was vomiting.

My heart could not carry this pain alone. If I had to support my husband after he confessed his adultery and carry my own grief by myself I knew I could not do it. I think at that moment my heart and spirit broke in a new way that I will never be able to explain. I think the parts of my heart that had separated during childhood separated again. I was shocked and unable to cope with the pain and grief.

It would appear that no matter what happened—if it was my childhood family or my adult family—somehow I was supposed to be the responsible one to acknowledge the fault and pain and clean up after everyone else. Would anyone ever be there for me and protect me? Was I never allowed to hurt and grieve and be comforted? *I needed a safe place to cry and be comforted.*

Then I remembered how I had asked my husband before I went to counseling if he had committed adultery. He had let me think our marriage issues were all about me and let me carry the weight.

I confronted my friend with whom he had committed adultery; I found out more information than what Patrick had shared. It was very hard for me to realize that my Prince Charming was withholding information from me. Surely Patrick wasn't like my abusive childhood family? I thought he was different and really loved me and we had just hit a low point in our marriage because of my struggles. I did not want to see that Patrick was anything less than the Prince Charming I thought he was.

Patrick promised he would never commit adultery again. I forgave him and believed that he would not be unfaithful again. We had some great times of love and connection, but it didn't last long. I believed that the Lord hated divorce and I did not want to lose Patrick. If I had not been a Christian I would still have done everything I could to save the marriage. I have a very loyal heart. I also did not want my son to go through the heartache of a broken family.

By the way, I still believe God hates divorce!

A year or so later I received a call from a close friend. She had something important to share with me and wanted to meet with me in person.

We met at the park and she explained to me that she had called my house one day and Patrick had answered the phone. Patrick had made a pass at her and she responded. Patrick had asked her if she wanted to come to the house while I was gone. She had responded with that would be nice, but she'd better not. She was confessing to me that she should not have responded even in word. Actions were not carried out, but I realized that, once again, if she had responded, more adultery would have happened, and with another of my friends.

At this point, my heart was broken with the reality of my past pain and now this new information that my husband had not changed. My counseling with Todd had continued, despite the misgivings I had after they shamed me into promising never to visit a bar again.

Basically I stuck with my Christian counselor, Todd, because I didn't want to start over and explain everything I had gone through up to this point to anyone else. I thought surely I would be healed and done with counseling very soon. Plus I felt I could do a lot of praying and basically the Lord and I could heal me if I just gave him the time to do it.

Right around the same time of my husband's second betrayal, Todd finally admitted that he felt my case had become too deep for him. I felt lost and hopeless back then. He recommended a counselor in California who knew and understood how the brain worked and the effect of abuse on the brain. Todd thought I could benefit spending a week with this psychologist.

Todd made plans for me to go to California to see Dr. Freeman. I was nervous, but I knew it was probably my last hope for someone to help me with whatever was wrong with me emotionally.

I was feeling more and more like a child inside. It was becoming harder to be a mother and making simple decisions became impossible. I knew I needed help when I was looking at all the different brands of orange juice at Walmart and I held my head in my hands and wanted to scream, "No more decisions!" **I knew this was an over-exaggeration of the present situation.**

I was working two days a week at a local restaurant at this time and taking care of my son and taking time out when I needed to journal and meditate on God's Word. I wanted our marriage to be restored and I wanted the healing I needed from my past.

I was in a constant state of anxiety living with Patrick. I didn't want to be anxious and I wanted to make it work, but I was an emotional wreck.

At this point I could hardly make it through two days of work each week. When I did work, I had to repeat Bible verses to make it through the day. "My soul finds rest in God alone" from Psalm 61 was one of my favorites. I was a server at the restaurant and after a couple hours of interaction with people I was overstimulated. I would try to make it through my shift through constant repeating of Scripture. At break time I would climb the stairs in the back of the restaurant to the attic to meditate on Scripture and beg the Lord to help me grow up and handle life on life's terms. After work I would go home and lie on the kitchen floor and cry for about thirty minutes before I could gather myself and go pick up my three-year-old son.

I stopped trying to figure out where the pain was coming from; it took too much energy. Instead I learned to lay with my face on the floor and just give him my pain. I would go get my son, bring him home, play with him, get him ready for bed and after he went to bed I was back to a prostrate position thanking God for getting me through another day. I would read the Bible and journal and simply be in God's presence. I would ask God to help me deal with whatever was going to come up the next day. Most generally he would not let me see into the next day, but what I wanted was to deal with tomorrow's pain today so I could just go through the next day pain free. The Lord never allowed me to dictate when and what pain would come out of my heart. I had to accept whatever happened. This was God's way of breaking me. As Oswald Chambers says in *My Utmost For His Highest*, God is making us crushed grapes and poured out wine for him.

I felt stripped of all the defenses I had set up in my mind to protect myself from the pain of my past. Now what? I had to deal with life and I felt naked and unprotected. I needed new defenses; they needed to be the Lord's truth.

As I write about this now, it's been many years since that time in my life. I don't understand how I made it. Only God knows.

Some principles that I learned through my healing include:

- His ways are higher than ours!
- The Lord never changes; he is the same yesterday, today and forever.
- He bought us with a high price and so our lives are not our own; they belong to the Lord, so he can do with us in this life whatever he wants.
- We are only renting these bodies and are here to be his hands and feet in the world.

I remember saying, as I was at the end of my rope with myself, my emotions, my marriage, my counseling, "Lord, I will do what you want me to do, and I will go where you want me to go, just carry me." Those weeks before I went to California I felt lost and alone. What was wrong with me? I thought Christian counseling could fix everything. So far I had been doing a lot of helping myself by journaling and asking the Lord to bring truth to the lies I believed and this was integrating the broken parts of my heart. The problem was that there were always more broken parts and memories. It felt like the birthday candle joke where the candles keep relighting after you blow them out.

I was tired and I was ready to give up on healing. Why had I started this process anyway? What was I thinking? I remember the reason I started the process was because I would see a glimpse of my broken heart and I recognized that it was soft and tender and I wanted to be like that all the time, and I made these great declarations to the Lord. *Word to the wise:* Don't make elaborate promises to the Lord, for he knows your heart.

During one of my times alone with my Lord, I said, "Lord, I want to live out of my heart, be the person you made me to be before my abuse/neglect. I don't care if I'm in pain all the time; I just want to live out of my heart." What in the world was I thinking? I do remember being tired of feeling like a shell of a person; however, *I did not count the cost before I made such a declaration.* I think the Lord took me up on it.

I also said something like, "Lord, I will do whatever it takes to be the person you designed me to be." I had no idea I was committing to a seven-year healing process where I would be hurt over and over again. Looking back, I was so naïve. The first week I spent with my counselor, Todd, I thought, wow, I'm healed! Little did I know it was only the first small layer which was going to open up everything else.

I remember at the end of the first week of counseling, I felt so new that when I begin to do laundry I had to think about how to do laundry. I couldn't remember. I felt like I was doing laundry for the first time in my life as a new person. This happened every time I had significant integration of past memories, or should I say parts of my broken heart, that would become part of me again. I had new perspective every time there was integration.

Integration was like a rescue mission. My heart had been broken into many parts and had been tucked away in a cold dirt cellar. As the Lord called these parts of my heart out of the cellar they became part of me and I gained their perspective. It was strange and exciting. As counseling went on and I could no longer count on Todd, I learned to do integration with just the Lord and me. I would bring my heart to him every morning and night and on weekends when my son was with his dad. I would ask God to rescue more of my heart if it was time. The Lord always rescued.

I could never get enough time with the Lord. I knew there was always more work to do. I loved spending time alone with him because I knew I would always be surprised. My friends could not understand how I could spend a whole weekend alone with the Lord. **I loved it and I figured the more time I spend with him the faster I would get healed.**

One of my favorite Christian bands, Casting Crowns, sings a song called "Praise You in the Storm." The chorus talks about praising God in the storm, and lifting hands to him, because he always holds us in his palms and never leaves us, even when our hearts are torn.

I would listen to this song over and over until I felt the Lord's arms around me. There are many other songs like this that I would play over and over until my sorrow lifted.

There came a time in my healing when I said, "*Okay, I'm done now. I'm done with memories, I done with the rescue missions. If there are more parts, let's just leave them in the cellar. I'm enough of a person now. I have enough of my heart to deal with. That's enough!*" **But the Lord never let me dictate my healing.** If he had, I would have been healed completely by that first prayer at the revival. Patrick's and my marriage would have been healed and we would have had more children and lived happily ever after. I didn't get my way.

Chapter Twelve
California

Well, they say California is the place you ought to be, so "they loaded up their truck and moved to Beverly." I still remember the old sitcom, *Beverly Hillbillies,* and their song before each episode. The year was 2001, I was twenty-seven years old, my son was almost four, and my husband Patrick and I had been married for six years. I set out on an adventure. *This recovering Amish woman had never flown or been to California.*

I was nervous, but at the same time it was my only hope to get help for whatever was wrong with me so I had to do it if I liked it or not. I flew alone and I was okay with that because if I did anything stupid at least no one who knew me would see. That was a comforting thought.

I drove two and a half hours to the airport and flew from there to California and, for the life of me, I can't remember where the connection flight landed and which airport I landed at in California. All I can remember is the different colors of people in California. I had never seen anything like it. Everyone was walking fast and cars were honking and moving fast. I was used to the clip clop sounds of slow-moving horse and buggies.

In California the traffic was a blur; I could not take it in. I stood in the street and stared at everything for quite some time. I don't remember if I used a taxi or a bus to get to the campus. All I know is that it was a fog, but that was becoming normal as far as my emotions, so I put one foot in front of the other and simply moved down the street. I had no idea where I was going, but I was going somewhere. At least I wasn't standing still.

Since I'm writing about 2001, it's a bit difficult to remember the details. I do remember the campus where I stayed and where Dr. Freeman's office was located. I was to see him approximately sixteen hours for therapy that week and I was looking forward to learning something that could give me hope.

The campus was an old one and the sidewalks weren't always even, so I had to be careful not to trip. There were many trees and picnic tables and Dr. Freeman's office was in an old building with wooden floors that shifted under my weight as I walked down the hallway. His office building was no longer used for regular classes so when I opened the door at the end of the long hallway it creaked and it was the only sound that echoed throughout the building. It was like I was in a movie and I would not have been surprised if a bat had flown out of one of the upper air ducts.

What was this counselor going to know? Would he be able to help me? I had tried to help myself; the church seemed clueless how to help.

The church left me with the feeling that if I really wanted to get better, I could. So the reason I wasn't better was because I didn't want to be better. Wow, if I really didn't want to be better and didn't know it, how sick was I? I thought with everything within me that I wanted to get better. Did I not know myself? Did others know more about me than me? I always found it interesting how my family and now the church would tell me how I felt and why I did or didn't do something. **I realize now that that was a form of control and no one should tell another he knows your heart or motives.** Only God knows hearts and motives.

On the first day of meeting Dr. Freeman my heart was pounding with fear and excitement and a small bit of hope. Dr. Freeman was a tall, gangly man with gentle eyes and an awkward smile. I would call him a little quirky. I remember the first day he said, "I want you to give up hope."

I dropped my jaw.

He said, "So you can have hope."

What? He had my attention. He was the only counselor who could stay ahead of me intellectually. Most counselors bored me because they would share things that I had already researched and discovered. I had a feeling Dr. Freeman knew a few things that I didn't know and I needed to listen carefully.

He proceeded to point out that my childlike heart was trying to hold on to the hope of reliving childhood in the right way—without neglect and abuse. *I needed to give up this hope and realize it was over and grieve the loss.* This in turn would give me hope to move on with my life as an adult.

Amongst many other things the two main principles I gained from Dr. Freeman were, one, "joy strength," and two, "return to joy." From his explanation I could tell these were my two main problems that led to emotional instability in my life.

Let me explain. I will use lay terms just so that I don't confuse anyone. Understand that there are technical terms for the brain that I'm not going to use. If you are interested you can read the books *Change Your Brain, Change Your Life* by Daniel Amen or *The Developing Mind* by Daniel Siegel. Both of these books will give you more technical terms than you want. If you want to read a book that is more in-depth about joy and the brain, read *The Life Model, Living from the Heart Jesus Gave You*, by James E. Wilder.

So, joy strength is an area of your brain that grows directly related to the stimulus you get in your environment.

It is absent at birth. This is why if you leave a child in a crib and don't interact with him/her, that child will not develop. Joy strength is like a muscle that grows, and it grows as people are glad to be with the person/baby, in this case. If a baby grows up surrounded by healthy individuals he/she will have plenty of joy strength to handle whatever life throws at him/her. Those of us who lack this joy strength have a harder time handling stress in our lives.

The degree in which one can suffer is directly related to how strong their joy strength, or their right orbital prefrontal cortex, has grown.

Return to joy, on the other hand, is how fast a person can return to a state of joy from the six emotional paths: shame, disgust, sadness, humiliation, fear, and hopeless despair. If a person can be ashamed and then return to a stable state within minutes they have a good return to joy circuit in their brain. However, those who were left alone in shame and pain and never shown the way back to joy from this emotional state may get lost and stuck in an emotion and have no pathway back to joy. This leads to addictive behaviors as an attempt to return to joy.

Bingo! These two problems were my problems. I could see it clearly as he explained how a person with joy strength and return to joy respond compared to one who has very little joy strength and lacks the brain pathways/circuits to return to joy from an emotional state. I started to view my emotional issues from a physical brain perspective and it gave me hope and changed how I viewed myself. It was not my fault that I was responding the way I was to life; however, I needed to find a way to change the way I was responding. I was determined to let go of some of the shame of my condition.

I knew that I encountered memories where I would get overwhelmed and I could not handle the memory on my own. I would get stuck and need someone to be glad to be with me and show me how to return to a state of joy. The problem, in light of this new information, was that the church and those who did not understand what I was going through were adding more shame to me while I was in pain and they were not helping me return to joy. They were shoving me further into the pit. No wonder I felt hopeless. I needed to surround myself with people who knew how to act when I went into shame or despair and could help me return to joy.

This process sounded so simple to me. I decided if I couldn't depend on people, then I sure could depend on the Lord to meet me where I was in the memories and he could be glad to be with me in my pain and help me return to joy.

I left California with a new hope that if I could get a few people to understand what I needed and the rest of the time I would ask the Lord to be with me, then I could fix myself.

I needed more joy strength and I needed to learn how to find my way back to joy when I was stuck in a memory. I figured if nothing else the God of the universe could show me the way back to joy. I also figured he could show me who I was in each emotion. Dr. Freeman pointed out that abused/neglected adults don't know how to act or who they are when they encounter different emotions.

The definition of maturity, according to the brain, is knowing who you are and what to do when you encounter all ranges of emotions. For example, when a mature person gets angry he still remembers it would be like him to love and respect another person during this bout of anger. Those who do not know who they are in the middle of anger will lash out and forget that they are hurting the ones they love. The immature person loses himself in the middle of the emotion and responds out of the back of his brain where he is simply trying to solve a problem. He is no longer relational; instead, he is trying to get this other person to be quiet, to stop the uncomfortable feeling evoked within him. *This is why conflict resolution becomes an issue when immature people forget that they are loving people first and foremost.* Instead, they lash out and then later, when they return to joy, they realize they blew it.

Mature people live out of the front of their brains and do what they prefer to do and they stay relational in the midst of conflict instead of treating the other person like an object.

My prayer after this enlightenment was, "Lord, please show me who you made me to be when I am angry, sad, and hopeless." I knew that I was not a mature person because the family who raised me was not mature, so I had no examples of maturity as I grew up. I had a strong faith and believed that it was still possible for me to become mature, have proper return to joy circuits, and to grow my joy strength in order to handle life. **I am living proof that an adult who is emotionally infantile with a weak joy strength can grow joy strength and return to joy circuits and grow up to be a functional part of society.**

If you recognize any of these issues in your life/brain, know that if God can take a broken infant like me, trapped in an adult body, and mature me, he can help you! *It takes submitting to God's path for your life, but it can be done.*

My typical day during the heart of my healing went something like this: I got up and read my Daily Bible, the book *My Utmost for His Highest,* and journaled about both. I would take care of my daily responsibilities if it was my son or my job and then, when my son went down for a nap, I would return to the Lord and I would praise him from hymnals. I would sit in his presence and drink him in. I knew this was the only hope I had of being a different person. In the evening after my son went to bed I would return to the Word and journal. I would ask the Lord about things that had happened that day that triggered an emotion. I would ask for truth and ask what the lie was that was bringing me pain. On weekends when my son was with his dad, I couldn't wait to sit in my comfy chair with the Lord and talk to him and find out what he had to offer me. What healing was he going to do in me today? I was eager to sit with the Lord like a young girl who was eager to spend time with her daddy. The Lord held me like a daddy.

I had shared with Dr. Freeman my desire to have a daddy and how I was completely consumed by it. He shared that it was dangerous to let this little girl run my life. I understood this, yet she was the most powerful thing within me and so I pleaded with the Lord to protect me from the wrong people who may take advantage of my pure desire for a daddy. I could see, as an adult, this could become a recipe for disaster with the wrong person as it had at the revival with the lay counselor. Dr. Freeman shared that my vulnerability in the wrong hands would be more pain for me and not be helpful whatsoever. My inner little girl needed to grieve the loss of her childhood, and not keep alive the hope of reliving it correctly.

Dr. Freeman said the hard thing was that it could take thousands of times for someone to show me how to return to joy before my brain found its own route. This was supposed to happen in childhood. The baby cries and the adult holds the baby and soothes the baby and she/he returns to a state of joy. As an adult spends time with the child and they smile back and forth, the baby's joy strength grows, and in a healthy childhood the baby grows good joy strength so he can handle life and return to joy from the emotions that life throws at him. Those who can't handle life and the pain turn to an addiction. This explains many addictions. The addicted don't learn how to return to joy without using a chemical.

As I discovered this information I thought I could figure out how to spend time with the right people and learn how to return to joy.

I shared with Dr. Freeman that I felt I was experiencing pain every day as I lived with Patrick because we were no longer connected. There was no joy or return to joy in our relationship and my brain, which was weak already, could not handle this disconnect. It triggered memories of my family life and it was too much for me to carry. I was constantly anxious and could not function when Patrick was around.

Dr. Freeman agreed that in order to save the marriage Patrick needed to move out and get some help individually for his infidelity and lying issues. Meanwhile, I could feel safe to deal with my own issues and then we could get back together when some of those issues were resolved.

I went home with a newfound hope that I could help myself and I might be able to get a few people in my corner who would want to be glad to be with me and help me return to joy. I knew that as a child my family was only glad to be with me when I was happy and when they could get something from me. When I was crying or upset they were not glad to be with me; they were angry and sent me messages of shame because they were ashamed. They did not have a return to joy from shame and pain, so how could they show me the way back? Instead, the response I received was anger and lots of physical shaking.

According to my memories I rarely felt comforted as an infant or child. This was the reason I was falling apart after my layers of self-protection were being removed. I had no foundation.

Chapter Thirteen
Return Flight

I felt the wheels of the plane as we picked up speed along the runway. My stomach was turning in part because of take-off and because I was leaving California to go home. I felt sick inside because I knew I could no longer stay with my husband and I wondered how our three-year-old would respond, as well as Patrick and his family. I could no longer think when I was in Patrick's presence. I felt everything inside of me was a jumbled anxious mess. I needed to be alone to heal with the Lord in safety.

Tears welled up in my eyes and spilled down my cheeks as the feelings of **complete failure** surrounded me.

"Lord," I prayed, "isn't there another way?" Other people stayed together and made it work. I knew I was going to be ridiculed by the Mennonite community for getting a separation and I wasn't sure if I could handle the shame in my weak state of mind. "Lord," I prayed, "I feel so naked, vulnerable, lost and all alone."

Before my healing began I was so strong, yet, was it really strength or was it just control? It was the bitterness that gave me a fake sense of strength. Underneath it all I was wobbly jelly with no feet to stand on.

My connecting flight was in Michigan or Minnesota, I don't recall which one, but the location was not relevant. What happened at the connection flight would forever be a mystery to me.

Before I went to California I was at a place where the current counselor, Todd, said he didn't think he could help me anymore. I couldn't continue to fly to California so I was not sure what was going to happen when I went back to see Todd, or if I was even going back to see Todd.

Who was going to help me? I wanted to be independent and the thought crossed my mind that maybe I could just do my own healing. The Lord could be glad to be with me, reveal truth to lies that were triggered and help me return to joy and become mature. Did I really need a counselor? It was so risky. If the counselors didn't understand they could hurt me more, could I afford more pain? I really did not think so, but I guess someone had other plans for me.

Let me share first before I tell you what happened at my connection flight. I still do not fully understand what happened and why it happened. If someone were to tell me a story like I'm about to share I would not have believed it and I would think he was lying, but nevertheless it happened. I have to tell the story because it just may help someone else; plus, I was in a crucial part of my healing and what happened changed me forever.

I was walking to my gate at my connecting flight and I looked up and who do you think I saw? The man I could not stand, Dr. James, the director of the counseling center back in my home state. The one who, six months prior, threatened to release me from counseling for my inappropriate behavior. It's strange how when someone you don't ordinarily care for becomes your best friend when you're both miles from home. The fact was, we were both from different states and he was flying from Iowa and I was flying from California and we both ended up on the same plane heading home.

Let me take a moment and talk about what I am feeling right this minute as I am remembering this story. I don't understand why God allowed this meeting and why he brought this man into my life.

Dr. James looked at me like I was his long-lost friend. I had never noticed his eyes before. They were sad like a little boy. Dr. James knew Dr. Freeman and when he found out I just spent a week with Dr. Freeman, he was eager to hear everything I had learned. Dr. Freeman was someone who had an edge on counseling and Dr. James was a fifty-four-year-old lay counselor who had graduated with every seminary degree possible who wanted to know more. I could tell Dr. James really wanted to hear what I had learned and there was a joy, a glad-to-be-together moment before we even got on the plane. We had bonded. I found myself very drawn to him, but not in a sexual way, just that I found him intriguing and his intellect stimulated me.

Hindsight says, if you feel emotionally bonded to a counselor in this way, run, don't look back, and don't ask questions, it's dangerous. No one should feel immediately bonded to a counselor; this is not healthy.

Dr. James suggested that he would ask the person next to me to switch seats with him once we got on the plane. This would give us an opportunity to talk on the hour and a half flight home. Now, Dr. James had flown from Iowa after board meetings with other counselors, and was connecting in Michigan or Minnesota and also heading back. I think the chances of a person flying from Iowa and a person flying from California to be on the same connecting flight back to our home airport is pretty slim to none. If a person tried to plan it, they probably could not.

Dr. James was the kind of person who, even if you didn't like him, commanded your attention just with his presence. I knew whoever sat next to me would move if he asked. Dr. James was a highly respected spiritual leader and was known for being able to help the worst cases, especially those who had come out of satanic ritual abuse. I was hesitant to share, but at the same time I thought, what could it hurt?

Dr. James took notes as I talked about joy strength and return to joy circuits and maturity. Somehow my previous notion of not liking him went out the airplane window and I *found myself feeling very protected and wanting to spend time with him.* I felt in my spirit that I should counsel with him even though I still had some reservations that I would probably get hurt again. So I shared this with him that I felt I should counsel with him. He seemed eager to do so.

After I came back home, we had a counseling session with Todd. I shared all my newfound information that I had learned from Dr. Freeman and then shared that I thought I should counsel with Dr. James. I told Todd that I thought Dr. James would hurt me, but I felt this was who I was to counsel with at this time. I wasn't sure if it was the Lord telling me this or if it was just my own desperate need to have someone help me. Todd and Dr. James both agreed and our first counseling session was set for July of 2001.

I knew Todd had said he couldn't continue to help me and my marriage was falling apart. Nothing was secure. I needed stability in my life and, on the plane, Dr. James seemed to want to be with me. He seemed like a different person than when I met him in the counseling center. This should have been my first sign not to counsel with him. However, I was like a ship lost at sea and if someone was eager to help me, I couldn't say no.

Patrick and I met with his parents to let them know about our separation. They did not think it was a good idea. At some point in the conversation Patrick's mom said, "Well, maybe if you would give Patrick what he needed he wouldn't have to go to another woman." I was shocked, but smiled and laughed nervously. Really, had I just heard what I thought I heard? Either way, I was sad because I had no relationship with my parents and because Patrick's parents had, in effect, become my parents, I felt I was losing more than I could handle. Yet I could not stay with Patrick at this time. I was an emotional wreck despite the years of counseling I had undergone. This should have been a sign to me that the counseling and therapy was not working. Yet I had no outside sources of influence or comfort or trust to turn to. I was desperate. I was a beggar and, as the saying goes, beggars can't be choosers. *Plus, the goal for the separation was not to end the marriage, but for both of us to have the space to deal with our separate issues and then reunite in the very near future.* I was hoping sooner than later.

My son was very upset. He was almost four at this time and he thought he was not going to see his dad anymore if we all didn't live in the same house. We explained to him that he would still get to see his dad.

The first time Patrick came and took my son for the weekend, they had walked out to the car when my son came back by himself and said, "Mommy, are you going to be all alone?" It broke my heart! I told him yes, but that it was okay, Jesus was with me. He bent over and started sobbing because I was going to be alone. I held him and explained that Jesus was with me and I was going to be okay.

This is still hard for me to think about because I know that children really suffer with separation and divorce. It breaks the heart of God and it's one of the many reasons God hates divorce.

Chapter Fourteen
Another Counselor

July came and I went to see Dr. James. I had been in horrible depression and was surrendering to it because I could not get back to joy. This was the state of mind I was in on our first session. I had not returned to joy in over a week and I was very sad.

At some point in the session Dr. James asked, "What do you think would help you?"

Without expecting a response, I said, "Well, if I could crawl up in your big lap and let God hold my little girl-self I think I would return to joy."

Dr. James always had a prayer partner with him in the room, and today was none different. To my surprise Dr. James said, "Okay, come sit in my lap."

I was shocked, but did not care because I had been without joy for a week. I snuggled up in his lap before he could change his mind or before I, as an adult, could reason through it. My little five-year-old inner self had powerful emotions and she was driving the bus that day. I can't explain this next part, but it happened. As soon as I curled up in his lap and his arms surrounded me, I felt warm from the top of my head to the tips of my toes and joy and light flooded me. Dr. James could feel it too and prayed for me. Now we were physically bonded.

Of course nothing sexual happened and so we both felt it was not inappropriate and it appeared that God had moved. I was shocked and couldn't explain it, but was so relieved that this time I had returned to joy again. I would get so scared of my memories because I could feel the emotion come up inside and then I was stuck and I never knew how long it was going to be before I would return to joy. I guess the reality was that I spent so much time out of joy that I hardly knew what to do when I was in joy.

I kept meeting with Dr. James and soon he started calling me on the phone and we would talk for hours every night. His pet name for me was Chickadee. He seemed to like who I was and didn't try to change me. He would say that he could see who I was going to be when I was healed and I was going to be a dynamic woman. I thought, yeah, right.

All I could see and feel at that time was that I was like a crying child. I was deeply ashamed of my needs and of my memories that would come up randomly. I felt like a child and had the needs of a child, like wanting to sit on a daddy's lap. It was humiliating. I longed to be protected by a daddy.

As I walked through the day I didn't know when the next feeling of being caught in quicksand was going to pop up. The quicksand represented my memories which were triggered by day-to-day life. It was a horrible way to live. Sometimes the memories were visual, where I could see them in my mind, but other times they were overwhelming emotions that I knew had nothing to do with any present day event. I prayed continuously asking the Lord to carry me and reveal truth. It took all the energy I had to make it through each day. I was fighting a war in my mind and heart, but no one could see it and trying to explain it in words does not do justice to what I went through.

I probably don't have to advise anyone to not sit on a counselor's lap, but just in case you are in a place as I was when this occurrence happened, never sit on a counselor's lap. It is not appropriate. It bonded Dr. James and me in such a way that I was blinded about where our relationship was going.

I have had second and third thoughts about leaving the above scenario in this book because I am humiliated by it. I have decided to leave it because it reveals the immature emotional state of mind I was in. I hope it keeps someone else from making the same mistake. Today, I can't imagine doing something like asking a counselor if I could sit in his lap, but I am not seeing things from that perspective anymore, thank the good Lord in heaven! I have lots of regret as I realize how my immaturity allowed me to walk into these scenarios. I was a very easy target. I made myself available and I was desperate. I made it very easy for others to use me and take advantage of me.

My actions said, "Please take advantage of me"; my heart said, "Please love me."

I wanted to be a five-year-old child and I wanted to be seen as a five-year-old. This is impossible when you are an adult. I was trying to make the impossible happen. It can't. After your childhood is over and you are an adult, all you can do is grieve it if you didn't get what you needed. You can't relive it and be healthy.

You will walk right into more abuse if you try to get those childhood needs met as an adult. I am living proof of this. **Grieving the loss of innocence and protection that every child should feel is very hard to do, but it must be done if a person who is emotionally childlike wants to grow up.**

Most people have never heard of this phenomenon and can't wrap their mind around it. Only those like me, who have actually gone through it, can understand the war that takes place inside the soul of an adult child.

The child feels trapped inside an adult body. These feelings can only be shared with a safe, healthy counselor who understands what is going on and does not perpetuate the problem and take advantage of the counselee's vulnerability.

Dr. James was very understanding when I could not return to joy and when I was stuck and needed help. He would call me and help me by listening to me and then when we were together he would hold me and let me cry. There were times when he said he felt like a child too and I would hold him and let him cry. He had dissociated parts as I did.

Hindsight says this is heading for disaster, but I couldn't see it and probably didn't want to see it once I was attached to him. I had so many people abandon me that when someone new would leave I would hemorrhage emotionally and could not handle the ending of a relationship. This caused me to stay longer than I should in most unhealthy relationships.

Soon Dr. James started sharing with me that his wife and family wanted nothing to do with him and that he had not gotten any presents for Christmas and his family didn't like him anymore. Of course this broke my heart and it roped me in.

In 2002, I discovered that my husband was still involved with pornography and when I brought it to his attention he lied. He called me the next day and told me the truth. I asked him why he had lied to me. He said he didn't want me to know what he was doing. I reminded him the reason for our separation was to work on our issues, not to continue in them. His reply was that he didn't think he had any issues, and that my issues were the problem. Now no one can argue that I had some serious issues but obviously, lying and sexual immorality were issues as well.

It had been a year since Patrick and I had separated and it appeared that he was comfortable in his life and things were not going to change. I shared this with Dr. James and he agreed it was time to write the obituary on the marriage. I asked to meet with Patrick and his parents and I explained that I didn't think there was anything left in the marriage. We proceeded with a divorce.

My heart was broken and my spirit was crushed. I didn't understand how we had lost our marriage. **I didn't even believe in divorce, so how was this happening to me?** Yet I knew we had reached a point of no return, trust had been broken so many times and Patrick did not think he had anything to change so there was no more work to do. I had been working on my issues from the past in hopes that as I dealt with my issues and Patrick dealt with his, I thought we would reconcile. I didn't want our marriage to end but I felt it was over already and I took the step to close the door to that part of my life and move on. I still wanted to believe that Patrick and I would be together forever and my son would not be raised in a divorced family. However, the writing was on the wall, it was over and there was nothing I could do to bring it back.

As I was grieving the divorce I discovered God's heart on divorce. **The Lord hates divorce because it tears hearts and bodies apart.** As I look back and write about it today, it still hurts. Divorce should never happen, but sometimes it does.

My editor asked me the question, "Why did you want to save the marriage when the trust, respect, and commitment were gone?" My first response to that question is why NOT save the marriage? When I married Patrick it was because I expected it to be forever. Yes, I believe that the Bible teaches marriage is forever. However, without this truth, I personally wanted to be with Patrick forever. I was a loyal person who wanted my marriage to be forever. I wanted my son to have brothers and sisters and for us to have a family who stayed together and prayed and played together.

I believe marriage is forever and if Patrick had given me

any hope that he wanted to work on his issues I would have stuck with him as long as I thought he wanted to change.

As I initiated the divorce I received many questions from friends and family on how could I do such a thing if I loved Patrick? From my perspective, Patrick ended the relationship when he decided to be unfaithful and continued in acts of immorality.

I chose to accept the relationship was over by initiating the divorce, but it was not what I wanted. I wanted to reconcile with Patrick, but his lifestyle was not reconcilable. So, as I grieved the loss, I was also ridiculed. This was very hurtful.

I felt I was standing beside the coffin of my husband, his family, our family unit and everyone was coming by and telling me how awful I was for ending it all. Yet, I felt I hadn't ended the relationship; I was simply accepting the obvious. While I was getting a divorce I still wanted Patrick, but even in my emotional state of immaturity I could see that it was over.

This broke my heart and I grieved alone with the added ridicule from others. No one seemed to be able to understand how I could want my marriage to last and still get a divorce. I cried out to God and let my husband go because I figured he would be happier without me, especially since he was not interested in living the lifestyle I wanted to live.

Little did I know that the divorce was going to open up unhealthy options in Dr. James's mind. Hang in there with me until Dr. James leaves and you will see how Patrick's and my divorce was not caused by my unhealthy relationship with Dr. James.

After the divorce was final, Dr. James started making sexual advances towards me. I asked him how he felt justified in this action since he was married. Of course, I didn't ask myself why I allowed it and didn't immediately report him to the authorities or at least my former counselor, Todd. Dr. James asked me if I felt dirty because of our sexual encounter. I had to admit that I hadn't. I actually felt soft and beautiful when he touched me, compared to when I was married to Patrick and I felt dirty during sexual activity. Dr. James said he was healing me from my past sexual abuse. It seemed to make sense and I let it make sense to me because it felt like the best thing that had ever happened to me.

The sexual touch spoke to the lies from my past and it was a return to joy for me like no other.

Please understand, this is how the devil can use our vulnerabilities to keep us in bondage. I could not understand how sexual intimacy in an adulterous relationship, even after what my former husband had done to me, could make me feel beautiful. And yet it was wrong. I had to believe what Dr. James was telling me because at that moment, he was in authority over me and my healing, and I felt I had no one else in my life I could turn to in order to discuss this situation.

Dr. James said we were having an Adam and Eve moment before sin entered the world. He would pray before and after each time we had a sexual encounter.

I struggled to make sense out of what was happening in this relationship that was supposed to be daddy/daughter. I prayed and I cried and I told Dr. James I was really uncomfortable with it. I felt God had led us together and he was helping me through memories. I was building joy strength and return to joy like I learned from Dr. Freeman, but now this one thing just didn't seem right. But I felt stuck since I couldn't bear to lose Dr. James. I thought I had to have him. I was feeling more beautiful and more emotionally intact than I ever had, so I concluded that we must be having an Adam and Eve moment as he said, and of course Dr. James told me not to share it with anyone. He said no one would understand.

Now, as I'm writing this, it makes me angry. Of course no one would understand because it was flat out sin. This is sickening to me now.

Another obvious sign that a situation is abusive, or at the very least, wrong, is when anyone asks you not to tell anyone else about your discomfort.

The day came when I was supposed to get my period and I didn't. We drove to a department store a half hour away to buy two pregnancy tests. Both were positive. To share how sick I had become, I was excited because I thought God had brought us together and this was his way of getting Dr. James to leave his wife and marry me. Obviously my thinking processes had become completely warped.

I remember the day when we sat on my couch and he looked at me. I knew him so well that I knew what the look meant. He wanted me to have an abortion, which he confirmed. What?! Was he kidding? Dr. James told me it wasn't the right time for a baby, and it was the only way to solve our "problem."

"But, how can we kill our baby?"

"Oh, no," he said. "We are not killing our baby. We are sending it to Jesus."

I am sick to admit that I died that day and chose a man over my child. I thought I had to have Dr. James. We were enmeshed and I could not live without him. Prior to meeting Dr. James I was weak and falling apart. While I was with Dr. James I felt a false sense of strength and I thought I was doing better. I could not afford to return to the weakness I had felt prior to my relationship with Dr. James.

So now I had done two things that I said I would never do: divorce and have an abortion.

About six weeks later, Dr. James came to my house and

said, "God has yanked my chain. I made you mine and you're not mine and now I have to let you go."

I was devastated. I could not return to joy from this. As I write about it now, it seems crazy that I would have wanted to be with Dr. James. I am nauseated as I write about such deceptions.

After Dr. James left, I told my friend Sherry everything that happened and she said I must tell the board of directors who were in authority over Dr. James. I can't believe it, but I told her that I didn't want to get him in trouble.

Sherry was adamant and explained that this man had used my vulnerabilities to get what he wanted. I still did not understand it this way. Sherry told me it was possible that the whole divorce was not supposed to happen and I needed to speak with Patrick immediately to find out what God might be doing in his life.

Sherry was the same friend who had responded to Patrick's advance towards her. She and I remained friends and are still friends today. Forgiveness and restoration of any relationship can happen when there is repentance. Without repentance some relationships are never restored, as the reader will see was the case with my divorce.

Sherry and I met with Patrick and explained what had happened. Patrick was angry and stated the obvious, that the doctor had used me and taken advantage of me. I was surprised to hear my ex-husband say that and wondered if it could it be true. My heart was so broken I couldn't handle the truth just yet.

I asked Patrick if the Lord was doing something in his life and maybe I had made a mistake and we were supposed to be together. Patrick told me that, no, he was finally enjoying life since he could play basketball when he wanted to and didn't have to go to church anymore.

Okay, well, there was my answer. I guessed I wasn't

wrong about the divorce. The interesting thing was that this was the very man who brought me to church in the first place. My, how things had changed.

Dr. James had removed a lot of people in my life and he was the main source of strength in my life. As a result, I was very unstable after he left. Sherry had to call the board of directors and explain what had happened. Dr. James was asked to resign and disappeared off into the sunset and I was devastated. I was still deceived and believed it was a Godly relationship.

To make amends, the board of directors set me up with another counselor, Dr. Stan. I was very leery, and didn't want another counselor, I just needed to get through this episode and move on. The board of directors understood my reservations, but told me they would cover the costs.

Chapter Fifteen
Not Another Counselor

D r. Stan called me and said how sorry he was that this had happened to me and I immediately let him know that I thought I was still to be with Dr. James and I was not interested in getting into another counseling relationship with anyone. I just needed a little help to sort this thing out and then I'd never sit in another counseling office again. I felt I could help myself better than all the counselors had so far.

Soon after Dr. James left, I was still very emotionally unstable and was forced to get help. I went to see Dr. Stan and another counselor they flew in, Dr. Polly. They felt a woman's perspective would be helpful at this crucial time in my life. Whatever, I just wanted to get back to joy and then move away from all counselors.

I spent sixteen hours with Dr. Polly and Dr. Stan and they both tried to reveal to me that I had sinned with this man. I told them I understood what the Bible said, but I believed that God had created an Adam and Eve relationship between Dr. James and me and we had not sinned. Dr. James had convinced me that we were having an Adam and Eve relationship before sin had entered the world.

As I look back, I wonder how I ever believed such a thing. Was it because I wanted to believe it? I was so deeply influenced by Dr. James that by the time he tried sexual acts I had to find a way to justify it.

At the end of the sixteen hours with Dr. Polly and Dr.

Stan, I admitted that I felt crazy because I knew it had to be sin, but I felt like it was not sin. How could this be? Dr. Stan and Dr. Polly did not shame me, but thanked me for being honest. I admitted that I felt very stupid saying that we hadn't sinned when I knew we had. Obviously I was having a serious disconnect between what I knew to be true and what I felt to be true. For those of you who like technical terms, this is called cognitive dissonance.

After the ten-hour drive home, I arrived home in despair. What was I going to do? I had been having crushing chest pains since Dr. James left and it felt like there was a strong spirit within me that made me feel like I had to have him back.

The next morning when I woke up I heard myself say, **"My soul finds rest in God alone, I submit only to the power and control of the Holy Spirit."**

I opened my eyes and realized something was different. I felt my chest. The pain was gone! The crushing feeling was gone! I felt light. I was scared to get up, though; what if the feeling of freedom changed when I got up? I reached for the phone and dialed Sherry's number.

"Sherry, you're not going to believe it, it's gone!"

"What is gone?" Sherry asked.

"The spirit, the heaviness, the need for Dr. James!" I told her. "I feel light, praise the Lord." I hung up and I went on my morning run, feeling lighter than I had in two years.

I called the contact I had for the board of directors and explained how the deceptive spirit left that morning when I was praying that I would only submit to the power and control of the Holy Spirit. I called Dr. Stan and shared the news with him.

Then it hit me. My eyes were opened and I saw that I had sinned. I fell to the floor in anguish. **I was grieved over my sin, but I was relieved that finally I was sane and saw sin**

as it truly was: SIN.

I thought back to when I met Dr. James in his office and then on the plane and how the progression of the sin happened. I was so desperate for help that I had allowed myself to be deceived and I had sinned.

As I write about it now, years later, I am still very sad and dumbfounded that all this happened to me. How does a person who loves Jesus, and is surrendered to Jesus, fall into such sin and not even think she is sinning?

I still shake my head and I am humbled that the Lord loves me enough to grant grace to this broken soul of mine.

If someone else told me this story, I would probably walk away and think they were lying. I know that I'm not lying and I know it happened to me, so I can't argue with it. *All I can say is God's ways are higher than ours.*

Dr. Stan, bless his poor heart, had to hear all my ranting and raving. *He was the only counselor who stood by me, did not shame me, did not use me, did not ever step over boundaries, but still showed love for me and my condition.* He believed me when I shared that I didn't want to be childlike. He believed me when I said I didn't know why I felt the way I did. He let the Lord work in my life and did not interfere when he knew I was steeped in lies. He prayed for the Lord to reveal truth to me and the Lord did.

* * *

If you haven't given up on me yet and you're still reading, it gets better from here.

Dr. Stan worked with me for about four years and then I flew away on my own. He told me the day would come when I would rather do something other than talk to him. I told him that would never happen. Funny, as I grew up it did happen just like he said it would. Dr. Stan was glad to be with me when I called and cried like a baby; he didn't shame me, and he showed me how to return to joy and how to act like a mature person when I was upset.

I will call his secretary Aunt Bea because she reminds me of Aunt Bea in the Andy Griffith show. Between Aunt Bea and Dr. Stan, over four years, I was parented in a healthy way and I will forever be grateful for the counseling and joy I received from both of them.

I would often call when it wasn't my time for an appointment, crying like a baby and begging to talk to Dr. Stan. Aunt Bea would pray for me and let me know that she would give Dr. Stan the message. I always felt they would help me if they could, and if not, the Lord would help me by myself and I would make it through the pain.

A healthy counselor helps you become independent, not more dependent upon them.

There were many times I felt like I could not go through one more memory of my childhood and survive. I would consider taking my life, but I would picture my son at my coffin, asking was Mommy never coming back? *I could not do it. I would keep this picture of my son in my mind as I cried out in agony from the misery of my past.* My son was conceived because God planned him for such a time as this. The Lord knew what I was going to have to walk through and that I would need a reason to walk through it. That reason was my son; I could not devastate him and leave him behind. So, I would beg God to keep me on the bed and I would scream until I fell asleep or the pain would subside.

Those years were healing, but I have to say I would never want to return to such a feeling of complete vulnerability. I felt so vulnerable when I was going through childlike memories and could not help myself. Of course it was painful, but it was also completely humiliating! Dr. Stan and Aunt Bea were so nice to me during those times of childishness, but I always lived in fear that one day their patience was going to run thin and they were going to yell at me and tell me to stop calling and grow up.

One night I had to have a conversation with Dr. Stan about how I felt he was going to die because he was leaving town for two weeks and I was not going to be able to talk to him. I knew better in my mind, but Dr. Stan's response was, "Well, it just means you're probably at a stage where you haven't learned object permanence yet." I thought this was ridiculous, since at that time I was thirty years old. Dr. Stan understood where I was at in my healing and he told me to embrace it and accept this was where I was at. This was hard to do, but necessary.

Dr. Stan had strict boundaries and would not give his cell phone number to his clients. I begged for it, but he never gave it. I was allowed to call his house number and listen to his voice and then leave messages if I needed to. But when he was out of town he was not reachable. After a while I was able to return to joy just by hearing his voice on the voicemail and then leaving a message and knowing he would eventually get it. It brought me comfort to know he would listen to my message.

Of course I couldn't share this problem with very many people because they would have thought I was crazy. I wasn't crazy, I was just immature and my brain was underdeveloped. After I understood this, it was easier to accept my condition; however, I was still humiliated.

* * *

I learned so many things while going through all that I

experienced and then trying to heal and become an adult. There are many people to thank for the freedom I have found.

Number one, I owe my healing to the Lord. Secondly, if Dr. Stan had not allowed himself to be a vessel for the Lord's healing, I may still be wandering out there somewhere feeling like a five-year-old and wanting a daddy to hold me.

Dr. Stan never held me. He simply was glad to be with me as I walked through my healing and I naturally grew up and away from the desire to have a daddy. I can't tell you how humiliating it was to sit in church and watch a daddy hold a daughter and to feel jealous. You just can't feel like this at age thirty and be okay with it.

Looking back, I wish I could have been a little easier on myself, but I just don't think I could because it was way too embarrassing. The Lord God was my personal daddy and helped me grow up. It took over seven years of therapy, but I finally grew up. Today I rarely ever get triggered into any memories of those abusive times in my life. I hurt over life and I will cry about the present, but it does not take me back to a dark, black hole like it used to.

So, how did I go from a five-year-old who wanted a daddy to an adult in a period of six years? I would have to say it goes back to the principles of the brain that I learned in California. I needed someone to be glad to be with me to build my joy strength and I needed someone to be glad to be with me in every emotion and show me how to return to joy. As Dr. Stan and Aunt Bea were glad to be with me in my painful childhood memories, they showed me the way out of the darkness into the light. I could never say thank you enough to these two wonderful people. They saw me for me and not just the broken down woman I had become. I have to say again I can't believe I survived all that. I just shake my head and wonder how all this could happen to one person.

I had two friends who stood by me; one was Sherry, whom I mentioned earlier, and then Tonya who was going through her own healing. They both saw me when I was very childlike and overreacted to life. Sherry taught me how to raise my son since I did not have any resources for parenting. I did not want my son to go through what I had and I needed a brand new template, so I would call Sherry almost daily to figure out how to be a mom.

Because I did not trust my parenting skills, I would pray for my son every day, especially while I was holding him. I knew I had lots of pain and demons from my past and I did not want my son to feel them from me. I wanted nothing to do with my past and I absolutely did not want to pass it on to my son. All I could do was pray that the Lord would protect my son from the evil spirits that haunted me. Of course then, when my son was not with me, I spent all my time with the Lord, begging him to heal me from all the lies and the evil that was still in and around me.

I would often want the Lord just to take it all at once, why wait? Now as I look back, I know that my brokenness was so deep that if the Lord would have brought light to all my darkness in one sweeping motion I would have been overwhelmed by the change. This would happen sometimes when the Lord did some major healing in me and I would feel so full of truth and light that it was uncomfortable. If a person is used to darkness for twenty years of life and then all the light is brought in all of sudden, it could blind him. The Lord brought the light as fast as I could handle it.

This is true for those of you who find yourself in need of healing: if you surrender to the Lord, he will heal you in his time, not yours.

A life verse for me is that God has bought us with a high

price and this is no longer our life we are living, but his (1 Corinthians 6:20). He can do with our life what he wants. If we are in pain every day of our life, well, then, let it be so. Someday all our pain and tears will be wiped away (Revelation 21:4), and this life is very short compared to all eternity. So, we have a lot to look forward to.

For the joy set before Jesus, he endured the cross. The joy was a relationship with us. If the Lord can endure nails in hands and feet because he wants a relationship with us, then we can suffer every day of this life and still have peace. We don't deserve to have a comfortable life. If we do, then we can thank the Lord, and if we are miserable in our life, it's okay, this is the Lord's life we are living. We have no right to say how his life will be lived through us. He died and bought us with his blood and now we surrender with open hands, not grasping our rights and desires, but living for him and him alone.

Our goal should be to please Him and only Him. This was a hard concept for me because I was always trying to get people to smile at me. I grew up looking at frowning faces and I wanted nothing more than to have people smile at me. If someone I looked up to was disappointed with me, I was devastated. We can't live like this and have peace. **If my peace is based on others, I'm going to be changing every day**. If my peace is based on God's truth and his truths alone, then I have a foundation that I can depend on.

Chapter Sixteen
Culture Shock

In 2006, I knew part of my healing would take place by moving away from my small hometown. I moved to a city where the population was over 100,000. It was a culture shock, to say the least. After working in the restaurant industry for the last thirteen years, I thought I had landed a job at a fine dining restaurant, but right before I moved I discovered the restaurant atmosphere would not work for me. There were some underlying issues that led to a hostile environment that was too familiar to my childhood. I had to leave the job even before I got started.

I found a job at a church as a facility team member. I was basically a glorified custodian. I carried a ring of keys and a radio on my hip. I was important, or so I thought.

The church did a fun night where they did makeovers. I was asked to participate. Growing up Amish I did not know anything about fashion, design, hair styles, or makeup. I was in my thirties and had never had my eyebrows waxed. I was shocked at how it brought out my eyes. I had my hair cut in a new style and makeup applied. I was quite stunning. It was truly a makeover and it was fun to feel beautiful. I remember going home and crying that night because I felt so beautiful and it was a feeling I encountered very seldom in my thirty years of life.

I had met a Christian man online who was from a neighboring state. I was currently renting a house while a family from our church was in Texas for missionary work. I decided this would give me some time to make a decision on buying in the city where I was living, or moving to the neighboring state where my boyfriend and his family lived.

After meeting my boyfriend's parents, we hit it off and I was open to moving to their city.

I did some comparison shopping. The cost of living in the neighboring state was cheaper than the city in which I currently lived. I prayed about it and asked the Lord to lead us in the process.

One weekend when I was visiting my boyfriend and his family, my soon to be mother-in-law and I went to look at a house. This was the first house I looked at. I had prayed, "Lord, I don't want to wander all over the place looking for a house. Please make it very clear if you want us to move."

I knew moving my son three hours away would cause a problem with his dad. I wanted to make sure it was really what we were supposed to do.

So we walked up to the door of the first house on our list. The door opened and I dropped my jaw. It was the worship leader from the local church where my boyfriend and I had been attending when I would visit. I told Ken that we loved the way he led worship and I was considering moving. He smiled and told me he felt led to start a church in North Carolina and had been praying that if it was God's will he would sell their house. We all stood there and I think we all had tears in our eyes because the Holy Spirit was speaking. Of all the houses I had seen online, I had picked this house first, so this had to be Spirit-led. I had my answer and Ken and his family had their answer.

The housing market was not good at this time; they had not had any offers, so it was most definitely a God thing. I offered them full price and we moved into a thirteen-hundred square foot home that was only five years old and very affordable for us.

Once again I was in the market for a job. Serving for thirteen years at the same restaurant was the only thing I had going for me. So I applied at local restaurant and I was hired. The first day of training was awful. They were so disorganized. I thought, "Lord, I cannot work here, please give me something else."

I was driving home from that first day and I looked up and saw a horse and buggy on a sign. Oh, maybe this is a sign? So I went into to the restaurant and was hired to work that very night. It was an Amish buffet, but it was not anything like the restaurant I had worked at previously. The owner knew nothing about the Amish, but he was using the name to sell his food.

I worked at the buffet for about two months and then one of the servers mentioned that a famous chain restaurant was coming to our city. I had not heard of this restaurant, but I thought, why not? I went to the address that I found in the newspaper. It was located in the mall and there were at least fifty people there trying to get a job. I told the lady who sat behind the applications, "I'm here to apply for a serving job?" I was hesitant because it was not what I was expecting. I was intimidated by all the people in suits and ties who were walking around. I had never been to anything like it. I timidly took an application and sat down to fill it out.

I thought I would come and fill out an application and leave it with someone. I had no idea that I would get an interview on the spot. The surprising thing was that I not only received one interview, but three. I was there for three hours.

At the end of the three hours I met a man who was tall and had warm eyes and talked real fast. I said, "Are you the doctor? Because I feel like I had a CAT scan and an MRI." He chuckled and I asked if he was going to tell me if I was okay.

We both laughed and he asked me what I would expect from them if I was to be hired. I said, "Respect."

He shook my hand and hired me. I couldn't believe it! I had no idea I was going to get a job the same day. Opening day was in a couple of months but we had extensive training before then. The menu had over two hundred and fifty items and we had to pass a written and an identification of dishes test by ninety percent or greater. I was quite nervous. We also had to learn how to present desserts and they had a special formula for how to greet and take care of customers.

I learned a lot about professionalism and I learned how to stand up for myself. I came into this restaurant a timid little recovering Amish, but I saw how everyone related to one another and I was being too nice. Everyone knew that I would not say no whether it was management asking me to work or a coworker asking for something from me. After a while I saw what was happening and I stood up for myself and actually grew up as well. I was probably at a teenage maturity level at this point and I slowly became my own person.

As I stood up for myself, I noticed that the managers respected me more. I became a trainer for new servers and I was good at training others.

Today I still call Dr. Stan when I need to bounce something off of him. I also stay in contact with Aunt Bea; they are both very dear, balanced Christian people who I trust for advice about life.

During my restaurant days I would call Dr. Stan and he would cheer me on, reminding me where I came from and how far I had come. It was always good to check in with him because he would remind me of what I had forgotten. He would remind me that I was handling a full time job and was functioning.

During my five years at this restaurant, significant

changes happened in my life. I would serve nurses who would inquire about my education and career choices. I had started back to school at a local community college majoring in Human Services, planning on working with hospice as a social worker.

I had also started volunteering with a hospice organization and I loved standing beside those who were dying and supporting them. It felt like it was my niche and that God was calling me to hospice. My son was now in fourth grade and I thought it was a good time to return to school and get a degree. I was done with counseling even though I still had triggers at times, but I was functioning and I could wait until I got home to deal with an issue. I could stay functional out in the workplace while I was hurting.

I served food to many nurses who would tell me that I had a nurse's heart and I needed to be a nurse. I didn't think I could ever be a nurse. In my mind I thought of them so highly and I just couldn't see myself as someone who could do such honorable work. I kept thinking of myself still as that little Amish girl who was nobody. My Amish family had thought I was nobody and *I still didn't believe in myself.*

I continued taking classes online and on campus while working at the restaurant. I kept hearing nurses say I needed to switch to nursing. Finally, one day the light bulb went on— God was trying to tell me something. I guess this little Amish girl could be a nurse? I didn't like blood. I felt the Lord telling me, "I got you, do it." I said, "Okay, Lord, I will give it all I have, but I need your help in order to become a nurse."

I switched my major and, unbelievably, I was accepted as one of the top sixty out of seven hundred applicants. I could not believe it, but I was accepted into the accelerated RN program at a local community college and *if I made it through, I was going to be a nurse in two years.*

Chapter Seventeen
Joy and Loss

After a year of living in the same city as my boyfriend and his family, he proposed in front of the entire church. I knew we were going to get married soon, but I did not know he was going to propose in front of the church. The worship leader, our church group, my son, and my husband's family were all in on the proposal. I was the only one who didn't know what was going on.

My in-laws were very excited to call me their daughter-in-law and I was excited to start a new life with my husband and his family. My son was eager for us to get married. My boyfriend and I did not live together prior to getting married and so my son was constantly asking when we were getting married.

We had a small fall wedding at our church with close friends and family.

My son had adjusted well to the move and found a great group of Christian friends at the public school he was attending. My prayers for his safety and protection were answered. I would be at home to see him off to school and sometimes he would be alone at home for an hour or so before I came home from work. This is the reason I had bought him a puppy—so he would not feel alone when he came home.

After my husband and I had been married for two years and I was taking my prerequisites for nursing school, I found out I was pregnant. It was so exciting, and the joy of telling the in-laws that we were going to have a baby was exhilarating. I told my son he was going to be a big brother and we were all on cloud ten. I had made a special treasure hunt for my son and the last clue was in his baby book, telling him he was going to be a big brother. It was so much fun, and everyone was ecstatic.

Everyone at the restaurant knew I was having a baby and there were at least four other co-workers pregnant. One day when I was standing at the cutting board to cut bread for my customers, I realized that something was missing within me. There was a presence I had felt since I had been pregnant and it was not there. I shook it off and went on with my night, serving customers.

The next week, right before my first ultrasound, I started spotting. My heart dropped, I had a feeling our baby had died. I called the doctor and they told me if I had more than spotting, go to the emergency room, but since my ultrasound was the next day, I could wait and come in the next day.

Well, I didn't make it. I miscarried in our bathroom. For the first time I looked at blood and it did not bother me. I saw it as life. I watched as I bled, and my heart broke. I tried to touch my baby but I could not find her. There was nothing I could do. We went to the emergency room and they confirmed there was no life inside of me. *There was no life in my uterus and I felt the life had gone out of my heart.*

The hardest part was to tell my son and my in-laws that our baby had died. My husband could not get in touch with his emotions; to him the baby hadn't seemed real. As a result, he said things that were very hurtful and my heart died even more.

I went back to work the next week and some people did not know that I had miscarried so they were asking me how my pregnancy was going. It was so hard to have to tell them I miscarried. By the third or fourth time someone asked, I wanted to scream and say, "My baby died, okay, and we didn't even have a funeral." It wasn't real to anyone except me.

I had to continue to go to work and see all my pregnant friends. It was torturous. All I could think was that I deserved to lose my child because the last time I was pregnant I had an abortion. How could I choose one life over another? I didn't deserve to have another child. Of course I had to have many tearful times with the Lord to learn truth over this very sad topic.

As I write about it today, I still am very sad that I chose a man over my child. I do not believe that it should be our choice to take our children's lives. *Our choice happens when we get pregnant, and we have no right to take our child or any child's life.*

As you are reading this today and if you're considering an abortion, I plead for you to look into adoption agencies. Love your child enough to give him or her a chance with parents who can't bear children. There is someone out there who will raise your child if you can't.

If you have had an abortion, the Lord forgives and healing can take place. Pursue a recovery program with others who have felt they had no choice. Healing is hard, but possible.

As I look back over my life up to this point, I would say my healing has taken place in a sense that I have more joy strength to handle life and remain functional, but I still hurt. My scars still hurt when I think about them. **It's hard to write about these stories of my life and not feel the pain. I do feel the pain, but what I do remember is that no matter what, the Lord has been with me.** I will go and be with him someday and these trials will have produced a glory that I can't understand.

I trust God's character even if I don't understand why I have gone through these experiences.

I started nursing school in the fall of 2010 and it was like what I imagined boot camp would be like. The environment was intense, the competition was intense, and the instructors were intimidating, trying to scare us. There were other students waiting for to take our place in nursing school. A lot of students didn't pass the first test. Great! Thanks for the encouragement. Nursing school cannot be put into words. You have to experience the sweat and tears to understand the testing and the load of information you're supposed to weed through to take a test.

Many times I thought I would not make it, but each time I survived a test and survived a clinical or class, I thought, maybe I can do this. On my first test I received a C. I was mortified! I had not received a C as long as I could remember. Thus, the work the Lord was trying to do in me through nursing school began. I was humbled. The Lord prodded me. Why was I so upset about a C? I had to look within and realize I was full of pride! Flat out pride. The Lord broke me during nursing school and once again my brain was rerouted and I became a new person.

As I write about these stories I realize how God has slowly morphed me into who I am today through all my experiences along the way. I would not be who I am today without all of these experiences. Would I really want anything about my past to be different? I would have to say since I've survived all of it and it has made me a stronger more mature person, I wouldn't want to undo any of it. However, that's just because I'm starting to experience the joy of suffering for the Lord. I didn't feel that way in the heat of the moments along the way. Suffering well means you become a better, more refined person after the suffering. **That is my goal throughout my life: that I would suffer well.**

I have not seen mature, godly, broken people who let the Lord use them, not have a story to share.

Usually the Lord has to squeeze the ugly out of us to make us into something beautiful.

Oswald Chambers says we can't be poured out wine and crushed grapes for others unless we surrender to the Lord's will.

As I enter my forties, I decided half of my productive life was probably over, so it was time to stop caring what others think and really do what God called me to do. I need to live each day within the Lord's presence and be his hands and feet no matter what he calls me to go through. I want to please him and obey him. "Don't let me come home a stranger," is my plea for the Lord, as the lyrics of a song by Fernando Ortega say.

My hope is that everyone who reads my story will find hope and realize that God is faithful and trustworthy, no matter how bad life becomes.

God is on his throne, he can be trusted when we don't understand his plan! We are not meant to understand his plan. We are only called to trust his hand as he moves us in our life. Our job is to stay open and surrendered so we can hear his voice and obey him. This life I'm living does not belong to me, so I can't decide what happens to me; I can only respond the way the Lord wants me to respond.

Willie J

One of my favorite life sayings is, "**It's not what happens to you but how you respond.**" This is truly the case. All bad things that happen to us or that we cause can be used for our best if we ask the Lord to grant us a heart of repentance. There is nothing so bad that God can't bring something good out of it, if we humble our hearts and bow before him.

Chapter Eighteen
New Career

I graduated from nursing school in the spring two years after I started, right on time. I couldn't believe I made it. Next I needed to pass the boards to become licensed. If I didn't pass this test all my nursing school efforts would be in vain. I had practice questions on my iPad that I took with me to my son's baseball games and then I had practice questions on my computer. I did approximately twenty-five hundred questions before I took my test three weeks after graduation.

I had been told that if the test shuts off at the seventy-five question point, I had either done real well or failed. I arrived at the testing site at six thirty a.m. when my test was scheduled for eight a.m. I wanted to make sure I got there on time. I sat in the car and did more practice questions.

As I did the test I was receiving a lot of "choose all of the following," and some of the questions I had never heard of the subject they were asking about. I was thinking, oh, boy this is like no other test I have ever taken. As I approached the seventy-fourth question, my heart started to pound and my hands got sweaty. Would my computer screen go blank after the seventy-fifth question? I had heard horror stories of how some people get all two hundred sixty-five questions. I did not want to be that one to get two hundred sixty-five questions and I did not want to be one of those who take the test three times and still didn't pass.

I answered the seventy-fifth question and hit next. My

heart stopped as the screen went blank. Was I really done? Had I passed? Did the last two years of hard work just come to completion; was I a nurse with a license? I got up and left. I called my friends from school since we had planned to meet when I was done and we really had no idea how long it was going to take me. I was done and I called them and squealed, "The test shut off at question seventy-five!"

We got together and of course we discussed how I felt throughout the test and I debriefed. There was a group of four of us who helped each other through nursing school and I can honestly say if it had not been for their support I'm not sure I would have made it. But we all supported each other and we all made it.

As I look back at that experience, once again I can see where God was working, allowing me to experience joy and support, and others being glad to be with me through a difficult experience. I was also able to offer my support to them and it was a beautiful thing.

Please, you must know if you have a hard time handling life, your joy strength can still grow today as people are glad to be with you.

The Lord has designed our brains in a way that truly sets us up for a need for community. We are not meant to do life alone. Our right orbital prefrontal cortex is absent when we are born and can grow and change as long as we live, based on the interaction we have with others. This is the area of joy strength, or you could call your "joy bucket." Some of us have an empty joy bucket and some have ones that are overflowing. If you have a full joy bucket, share it with others. It's a gift from God and joy should be shared.

After I met with my friends, we checked the website to see if I had a license number. It was still pending. I drove home, and when I arrived at home, I checked the website again and I had a license number!! Unbelievable! I was a licensed RN! My husband and my son where there and we celebrated.

The next day, I had an interview with a local hospital for a position in their progressive care unit. I got all dressed up in my uncomfortable shoes and went to my interview with my license number. I had memorized it already and announced it to the person who interviewed me. The person interviewing seemed impersonal, so I left thinking, well, they won't be calling me.

I stopped at another hospital on the way home and left a note for the manager who I had spoken to a month prior. When I was almost home, I got the phone call. The local hospital offered me the job I had just interviewed for. I was truly shocked. I said yes, of course, and was told I could either start orientation the following week or wait until the next month. I decided sooner than later. I finished the paperwork and started the following week.

This meant we could now sell our small house and buy a bigger one. We had an immediate offer on our house and we accepted. Then we became buyers.

My husband had a good feeling about one of the houses he had seen. After one of my son's baseball games we drove by the house. We called the Realtor and she invited us to knock on the door and see the house. The Realtor informed us that the sellers were trying to sell because they were going to Costa Rica to be missionaries. By the end of the week they were going to take the house off the market and be forced to rent the house.

Sure enough, out of routine, we went to meet this couple and see the house. My son was like, "You guys don't have to pray about this. You know this is our house." It had a fenced-in yard which we needed for our two little dogs and my husband needed an office for his business he did out of our home. Everything was perfect.

We proceeded with the loan process and discovered I would be right on the edge of not being able to provide proof of employment with two paychecks from my new job. It all worked out in the end and we closed in July.

A lot had happened since I graduated in May. My life was no longer recognizable. The new house, new career, and even a new car, was a whirlwind and I survived.

As I look back, I realize once again how each step of my life brought me to a place where I could handle all these changes without falling apart. Amazing, as I think about all that has happened in my life. What will my next forty years look like? Only God knows.

My emotional healing lead me to a place where I could help others like I never imagined I could. Working my new job in a hospital as a RN was surreal to me. I never dreamed I would be able. Still, two years later, I have to pinch myself to see if it's real.

Let me share a story that happened one day on my job that shows how much I've grown.

Sometimes I think I could write a book just by writing what happens to me daily and what the Lord is doing. It was a Friday and it was the last twelve hour shift for the week. As I was driving down the street, two blocks from the hospital, this wave of emotion hit me. I had been talking to the Lord as I usually do on my twenty-five minute drive to work. I was thinking about the years I lost, or felt I lost, due to the abuse I experienced in my past. It was just now at age thirty-eight; I felt I was finally experiencing life as it happened. I was living in the moment, I thought, as I was making the turn at the light. I was a nurse and learning new things every day and actually living in the present. I did not have to go home every night and process triggers of painful memories of the day that brought up past issues, and spending three hours a night revisiting my past. I was really thriving. "It's about time, Lord!" I started to cry and then I got that ugly cry going on, like Beth Moore talks about.

I looked in the rearview mirror and thought, oh boy, I was actually looking good this morning and now my mascara was running. But then I didn't really care because I was finally living in the moment. What an awesome feeling. I praised God and told him how blessed I felt that I was able to be a nurse and live in the present.

The above experience may not be that significant had the day not unfolded the way it had.

I had been asked once again, as I had the day before, to work on the unit across the hall. I work in a specialized unit where we get patients who no longer need to be in the ICU or need more monitoring than a normal med surge floor may be able to provide.

During report I could tell it was going to be a very busy, trying day. I would have three patients, one of which needed a blood transfusion before his procedure at noon. I thought to myself, this is going to be impossible. When transfusing any blood products vital signs must be taken at the beginning of the transfusion and the nurse is to stay in the room for the first fifteen minutes and then take vitals again to ensure that the patient has not reacted to the blood product. So, take this process times five and I wondered how I was going to take care of my other two patients. "Lord," I prayed, "you will provide a way."

So with great confidence and with my inspiratory moments with the Lord that morning, I was just glad to have this challenge. I had a great perspective and attitude.

I had been with this patient the day prior for twelve hours so we had a connection already and I was very familiar with the treatment plan. I was comfortable—too comfortable. I saw that his IV bag was almost empty and I thought about changing it.

I knew this bag was located in the fridge, where very few bags of IV need to be. I grabbed it without looking at the label to verify that it was the correct bag with the correct name on it. This was my first mistake. Nursing 101 is always, always, read your labels of all meds and make sure they match the patient. So I made my first mistake because I was comfortable and thought I knew exactly what I was doing. I can see my nursing instructor's face in my mind when I think of this mistake. Her face would have a look of disgust and her finger would be in my face. I shiver to think of it.

Next, I log in to the room computer and try to scan the bag, still not looking at the patient's name or med label. It doesn't scan; I was not surprised and remembered it had not scanned the day before, either. This was my second mistake. I hung the bag anyway, thinking all the while about my infusion deadline and that I would be the nurse who could make it happen.

I was interrupted many times by other doctors having questions about my other patients. I prioritized my day from the most important tasks to least important and I thought the day was going well.

Soon after my patient went to have his procedure, we received a call that the doctor wanted to transfer the patient to another area of the hospital after recovery. He stated he thought the patient would be better cared for on the other unit. I didn't know if it was personal but I took it personally. I had worked so hard to get his transfusions complete before he went to his procedure and now they were going to move him. My feathers were slightly ruffled but I kept my feelings to myself.

Protocol is to call a report to the nurse on the other unit. I documented the report and informed the family that the patient had been moved.

An hour had passed and I was passing time with a mandatory computer learning program I had to do.

I received a call from the nurse I had given the report to. She asked me if I had an order to transfuse calcium gluconate on the patient who was transferred. She informed me that the calcium gluconate was transfusing with another patient's label on the IV bag. My insides fluttered, I think the color drained from my face, and I said, "Really? That was for my other patient." This was a real elementary mistake. I hung up the phone and thought, what do I do?

Our manager was in the station at the time and I thought, I really need to go tell her, but will I get fired? Have I hurt the patient? I couldn't believe this was happening. I got up with wobbly legs and approached my manager. I just found out I hung the wrong med for the patient I transferred. I thought I was going to vomit; the idea of what could have happened was almost too much for me. The manager and I started looking at the patient's labs and discovered the patient's calcium was low and he would have needed the calcium. My manager informed me that at times they give calcium to patients who get a lot of blood due to possible clumping.

I was dumbfounded and overwhelmed as I realized in my busyness and complete failure, the Lord had my back. Wow, I am still shocked that I missed the basic steps of med administration not once, not twice, but three times! And God allowed me to pick a med the patient could actually use? What are the chances of this? None! It's a miracle. The same way it's a miracle that I survived my childhood and became a functioning part of society.

Today I feel waves of shame as I think of what I did and then I'm overwhelmed with God's grace and mercy that he would so love me that he would have my back when I failed miserably.

All I can say is that God was teaching me that I didn't have to be perfect and he still loved me. I wish I had learned this growing up. I so long for acceptance and affirmation and never received it from my family. I've been reading this book called *So Long Insecurity* by Beth Moore and she stated in her book that one of the reasons we try to be perfect is because we want to be the best and want to be noticed and affirmed. This is so me. I have beaten myself up all these years, trying to shame myself into perfection and all along I didn't need to be perfect. I have wasted so much energy on trying to be someone I'm not.

"Forgive me, Lord, and help me to be a humble example of your undeserving grace. I will do a better job in life if I relax and not seek out affirmation. Lord I will let you keep teaching me that I can rest in you and let you give me strength. I have none.

"Lord, let me never ever forget this lesson I learned yesterday. May it serve as an example to all who hear about it. You care about us when we try to do life in our own strength and fail miserably. Your undeserved mercy and grace is more than I can comprehend. Lord, remove some of those old lies that lie on the dusty shelf of my mind and make room for your tender Fatherly love that cannot even be put into words."

Chapter Nineteen
My Surgeries

After I started my new job and had health insurance, there were a couple of things I wanted to get checked out. The main issue was my neck pain. It would shoot up into my head and neck, down around my shoulder blade and down my arm into my hand. I knew from the description of the pain that it was nerve pain, but why was it there and what could be done about it? I had neck pain for many years, but in the last year the pain had driven me to tears. I knew it was time to look into the source of this pain.

I went to my new family doctor who wanted me to try physical therapy first. So I went to three months of therapy and it helped during therapy, but the pain returned. We tried a muscle relaxer. I went to a chiropractor who was not covered under insurance and he took an X-ray of my neck. The chiropractor's opinion from the X-ray was that I had herniated discs in my neck, but without an MRI this diagnosis could not be confirmed.

I was doing stretches that my physical therapist gave me to do when a pain so sharp that I could not get up off the floor brought me to immediate tears; it shot through my neck and down my arm. It felt like a guitar string had broken and it was causing severe shooting pain.

I went to the ER and they did an X-ray and gave me pain medicine. I requested an MRI. The ER doctor did not think the X-ray revealed anything significant and did not order an

MRI. The doctor wanted to send me home with pain medicine. I told him I was a nurse and was not interested in taking daily narcotics. I went home frustrated.

I called my doctor and requested an MRI. The insurance would not cover it. They wanted me to try physical therapy again. I was so frustrated. Here I was in the health care field where I advocated for all my patients, but I could not advocate for myself. I knew something was going on with my neck and it was more than what a chiropractor or physical therapist could fix.

I called the insurance company and I explained my predicament and frustration. The chiropractor sent a copy of the care I had received from him and within days my MRI was accepted. The MRI revealed that I had five herniated discs and a bone spur pushing on the nerves in my neck.

The chiropractor recommended a well-known neurosurgeon who worked at the hospital where I worked.

I met with the surgeon who was surprised at the state of my neck. I wasn't even forty, and could not point to one thing that had caused my problem. Then my mind went to my abuse from my brother who used to stand me on my head, and I wondered if the deterioration started then.

The surgery was scheduled to remove two of the herniated discs. It was a common surgery recently coined the Peyton Manning surgery. My mother-in-law and my sister-in-law both had this same surgery. This seemed odd because we were not related, but were all having the same surgery within a year of one another. I love to joke with my husband and so I told him the only common thread between me and my in-laws was him. So the cause must be him. He must be a pain in the neck, causing all the women in his life to have pains in their neck. My mother-in-law, sister-in-law, and I had a great laugh.

The plan was to be off work for six weeks due to a weight

restriction of not being able to lift over ten pounds. The surgeon said I would probably feel so much better without the pain that I may feel ready to go back to work before the six weeks. I had high hopes for a fast recovery.

Much to my disappointment I had more pain after surgery and not less. I had registered for online classes to receive my Bachelor of Science in Nursing degree. I poured myself into my online classes and was focusing on studying and trying to ignore my neck pain.

I started post-op physical therapy four weeks after my surgery and each day the pain was worse after therapy. I was really frustrated and it was not like me to admit that I was in pain and that something was not right.

I called the surgeon's office and shared that something was not right. I felt like someone had implanted a bug zapper into the left side of my neck and it was zapping me in a C shape from behind my left ear down to my shoulder blade. I would try to ignore it, but it would not let me.

I went back to the surgeon and I described what was going on and he said we needed to do another surgery to remove another disc. He shared his hesitation because it could cause swallowing problems and he did not like to do surgery on that area.

Great, I thought, I'm going to have a feeding tube.

The surgeon shared that we could try a nerve block first, which would be less invasive and some patients have received relief for years from the nerve block. I was all for that because it would mean I wouldn't have to be off of work for another six weeks.

I called my boss and explained that we were going to try the nerve block and see if it worked and if it didn't, I would have to have another surgery and would be off another six weeks after surgery. I was disappointed and felt like I was letting my boss down. She was supportive and wanted me to take care of myself so that whatever needed to be done would be done the right way before I came back to work.

The nerve block was placed and I woke up with no pain. I was so thrilled, I told the surgeon I loved him and thanked him. He warned me that the reason I felt no pain was because my neck was numb, but once the numbing agent wore off I would have some pain. However, within twenty-four hours we would know if the steroid shot had worked.

On the car ride home, I felt every bump and my neck pain came back with a vengeance. The pain was so overwhelming that I could do nothing but cry. I felt defeated.

Then next day I woke up and the pain was manageable and I thought this may be working. The following day I had less pain and I said, yes, it worked. I did not waste any time to call my surgeon, my boss, and employee health office to tell them I was coming back to work. I had to go to employee health and fill out some papers saying I was ready to go back to work.

Two days later the pain started coming back. I was devastated. I had cried wolf. I called my surgeon and we scheduled the next surgery.

Once again I had to call my boss and employee health office to tell them I would not be coming back until six weeks after the next surgery. I was unable to work for fifteen weeks.

The only way this could be a good thing was if I could get most of my thirty-nine credits I needed for my bachelor's degree done and out of the way during my time off. I decided I was going to put my nose to the grindstone, and getting my degree became my priority in the middle of icing my neck and putting heat on my shoulders and doing stretching exercises.

The second surgery was successful and I had more pain than I did after my first, but they had warned me that the muscle spasms would be very painful due to having two neck surgeries in two months. The first two to three weeks after the second surgery was absolutely miserable, but I lived to tell about it.

During this time, my son's travel baseball team had planned a trip to Florida. I was in so much pain and yet I could not miss my son's trip to Florida and his sixteenth birthday, so I sucked it up and went. I had a neck brace on most of the time and I looked like a fruitcake, but I was there.

The best part is that by December of that year I had completed thirty-nine credits and received my Bachelor of Science in Nursing.

I had felt so worthless while not working that I had to do something or I would have lost my mind.

I know I have some healing to do in this area because I should not find so much of my identity in working that I feel worthless when I can't work. However, in this situation it worked in my benefit because it drove me to work hard to get my bachelor's degree.

One year after my second surgery I started having nerve pain down my arm again. After two steroid injections and a MRI, another surgery repaired another herniated disc in my neck.

I have one more herniated disc in my neck that has not been repaired. I am keeping my fingers crossed that it will not need repair. Most generally neurosurgeons do not repair herniated discs unless it is causing significant pain or weakness. This is the reason I have had three neck surgeries. It is not protocol for a surgeon to repair multiple herniated discs at one time unless it does not restrict mobility for the patient's neck.

A decade had passed since my encounter with Dr. James. A friend of mine found some information that broke my heart. Dr. James was a pedophile. I had been deceived by not only an immoral man but a pedophile. I spoke with his daughter who Dr. James had molested and I was sickened to find out the truth about Dr. James. I knew he had many issues but to find out he was a pedophile long before he deceived me was really hard to stomach.

It's hard to see how when we are abused as a child we seem to seek out and draw those who are like those who hurt us. If you ever feel drawn to someone and deeply connected in a matter of minutes, I would double check the reason behind this. It could be healthy, but I would venture to say that there is something unhealthy connecting you to someone. Take this sign as a red flag and ask someone else about this person.

If you notice that you are overly consumed by thoughts about a person and want to talk to that person a couple times a day, this is probably not healthy. Take a step back and don't talk to that person for a while and focus on prayer. If you are supposed to be in relationship with someone, that person will remain in your life. **Don't cling to any relationship except your Lord.**

Chapter Twenty
Empty or Fulfilled

When my only child received his driver's license, I was not prepared for the emptiness that it brought to my heart. I walked him out to his car that first day and he said, "Mom, it's like you're walking me to my bus."

"Yes," I said, "I can do that if I want to." I hugged him and told him to be careful and watched as he drove away. I watched until I could no longer see his car and then I just stood there.

I went upstairs to my serenity room and I sank down into my comfy chair. I felt empty and useless. The only thing my son needed me for now was food and money. He could drive away by himself now.

I prayed through this and am still praying through this because my identity should be found in the Lord, not in being a mom, or a wife, or a nurse.

In the days after my son started driving, I wondered about my purpose in his life. I had been a nurse for two years and a mom for sixteen, and I was wondering about my purpose?

I thought nursing would satisfy my desire for a career and then I became a nurse. Why was I wondering about my purpose in life because my son got his driver's license and in a small part, his independence? I realized there was a problem with my thinking.

Do I find too much fulfillment in things other than the

Lord, and therefore I change how I feel about myself based on what is going on in my life? This is no way to live a life.

It's interesting how I can say all the right things, but life reveals what is going on in my heart. Incidents in life don't cause us to feel or think or certain way; they simply reveal that our hearts.

This incident with my son revealed that I have some work to do on finding out my true purpose in being a child of God. That should be enough, a job, a child, a perfect husband...

Anything that is temporary is not going to fulfill us. Our relationship with our creator and our identity in him is what should fulfill us.

I'm going to guess this is an area I will struggle with the rest of my days here on earth. I think the Lord has healed me from my past to a certain degree. I had hoped I would reach a place of complete serenity and peace with no more struggle. I don't think that is a realistic goal for any of us. We all have a past; our memories and pain are on different levels, but nevertheless, it is pain.

I believe part of keeping us humble and dependent upon the Lord is to keep it real. We are human beings who have been hurt and we long for love. Some of us have not received, or will never receive on earth, what we had hoped for. However, the joy and glory we will receive in the next life will far outshine anything we could have dreamed up in our hearts here.

My hope for my future is to continue to mature as a woman, as a Christian, as a mother, and as a wife. Hopefully someday I will have the joy of having grandbabies. I will spoil them and send them home. I still desire to work with hospice and hope to do so after I have worked at the bedside for five years. I am teaching myself to play the piano and want to play for my hospice patients. They may be the only ones who will like my music.

I do love to sing, but I can't carry a tune in a bucket. One day at work I was singing to a hospice patient. I had only started humming and the patient said, "Stop singing, you're going to start my hell early." I had no idea my singing was that bad and can only laugh when I think about it.

Let me remind you that the Lord is working in our lives even before we know him.

Let's recap:

- The Lord gave me a desire to run and allowed me to get hooked on endorphins instead of street drugs.
- He reminded me through my friend that I would never see my niece again and therefore I went back home and finished school.
- He kept me from taking my own life by giving me my son.
- He protected me by bringing Patrick into my life so that I didn't run off to Chicago.
- He brought John and Frieda, who were the first ones to tell me that I did not have to be Amish to go to heaven. I may not know Jesus today if they hadn't informed me of this important fact.

All the above things happened before I met Christ.

I desire to motivate many women to hope and trust in the Lord in spite of their circumstances. My message to everyone reading this is it's not what is happening to you, it's what you're doing with it. If life gives you pineapple juice, drink it and enjoy it, but if life gives you lemons make the best lemonade anyone has ever tasted. Don't become bitter.

Willie J

Forgive and let go and let God. God is a just God; he will take care of those who are abusing others. We don't have to vindicate ourselves. In due time all secrets will be revealed and truth will stand the test of time.

Appendix

Principles Learned With Scripture

Those who abuse/neglect others are in more pain than the one who has been abused. We must ask the Lord for compassion towards those who inflict pain.

Matthew 18:6-7 *THE MESSAGE*

But if you give them a hard time, bullying or taking advantage of their simple trust, you'll soon wish you hadn't. You'd be better off dropped in the middle of the lake with a millstone around your neck. Doom to the world for giving these God-believing children a hard time! Hard times are inevitable, but you don't have to make it worse—and it's doomsday to you if you do.

Suffering well means that we are able to look to the Lord in our suffering and become a more mature Christ like person.

James 1:2-4 *THE MESSAGE*

Consider it a sheer gift, friends, when tests and challenges come at you from all sides. You know that under pressure, your faith-life is forced into the open and shows its true colors. So don't try to get out of anything prematurely. Let it do its work so you become mature and well-developed, not deficient in any way.

The Lord longs to be with us and help us with our struggles. If you will just lift your chin towards him and say okay Lord if you are who they say you are, please reveal yourself. Give the Lord an inch and he will take you many miles into his peaceful presence and truth.

Luke 13:34 *THE MESSAGE*

How often I've **longed** to gather **you**r children, gather **you**r children like a hen, Her brood safe under her wings— but **you** refused and turned away!

2 Chronicles 16:9 *New Living Translation*

The eyes of the LORD search the whole earth in order to strengthen those whose hearts are fully committed to him.

We all have the same struggle against the same sinful nature. What we feed will grow. Feed the sinful nature and your life will reveal the fruit of anger and selfishness. Feed the Holy Spirit and your life will produce the fruit of the spirit such as self-control.

Romans 8:5-8 *THE MESSAGE*

Those who think they can do it on their own end up obsessed with measuring their own moral muscle but never get around to exercising it in real life. Those who trust God's action in them find that God's Spirit is in them—living and breathing God! Obsession with self in these matters is a dead end; attention to God leads us out into the open, into a spacious, free life. Focusing on the self is the opposite of focusing on God. Anyone completely absorbed in self-ignores God, ends up thinking more about self than God. That person ignores who God is and what he is doing. And God isn't pleased at being ignored.

Romans 7:18 *New Living Translation*

And I know that nothing good lives in me, that is, in my sinful nature. I want to do what is right, but I can't.

Galatians 5:17 *New Living Translation*

The old sinful nature loves to do evil, which is just the opposite from what the Holy Spirit wants. And the spirit gives us desires that are opposite from what the sinful nature desires. These two forces are constantly fighting each other and your choices are never free from this conflict.

Galatians 6:8 *New Living Translation*
Those who live only to satisfy their own sinful nature will harvest decay and death from that sinful nature. But those who live to please the Spirit will harvest everlasting life from the Spirit.

We exist for The Lord; he does not exist for us. He is pleased with his creation.

Revelation 4:11 *New Living Translation*
"You are worthy, O Lord our God,
to receive glory and honor and power.
For you created all things,
and they exist because you created what you pleased."

God's ways are higher than ours and we don't have to understand, because we are not God.

Isaiah 55:9 *New Living Translation*
For just as the heavens **are higher** than the earth, so my **ways are higher** than your **ways** and my thoughts **higher** than your thoughts.

This life we are living is the Lord's life because he bought us with a high price, his precious blood. We don't have the right to say how the Lord lives through us. We surrender and ask for the privilege to be his hands and feet as a way to thank him for saving us.

1 Corinthians 6:19-20 *New Living Translation*
Don't you realize that your body is the temple of the Holy Spirit, who lives in you and was given to you by God? You do not belong to yourself, [20] for God bought you with a high price. So you must honor God with your body.

The Lord draws us; we can't even come to him without his help.

John 6:44 *New Living Translation*
For no one can come to me unless the Father who sent me draws them to me, and at the last day I will raise them up.

The Lord expects us to walk with him and let him help us.

I like both versions NLT and *THE MESSAGE* for the following:
Micah 6:8 *THE MESSAGE*
But he's already made it plain how to live, what to do,
what GOD is looking for in men and women.
It's quite simple: Do what is fair and just to your neighbor,
be compassionate and loyal in your love,
And don't take yourself too seriously—
take God seriously.

Micah 6:8 *New Living Translation*
No, O people, the LORD has told you what is good,
and this is what he requires of you:
to do what is right, to love mercy,
and to walk humbly with your God.

The Lord considered it a joy to have nails in his feet and hands so that he could have a relationship with us. We must be important and valuable.

Hebrews 12:2 *New Living Translation*

We do this by keeping our eyes on Jesus, **the** champion who initiates and perfects our faith. Because of **the** joy awaiting him, he **endured the cross**, disregarding its shame. Now he is seated in **the** place of honor beside God's throne.

Suffering in this world will be nothing compared to spending all eternity with the Lord.

James 1:12 *New Living Translation*

God blesses those who patiently endure testing and temptation. Afterward they will receive the crown of life that God has promised to those who love him.

Hebrews 12:11 *New Living Translation*

No discipline is enjoyable while it is happening—it's painful! But afterward there will be a peaceful harvest of right living for those who are trained in this way.

2 Corinthians 4:17-18 *New Living Translation*

For our present troubles are small and won't last very long. Yet they produce for us a glory that vastly outweighs them and will last forever! [18] So we don't look at the troubles we can see now; rather, we fix our gaze on things that cannot be seen. For the things we see now will soon be gone, but the things we cannot see will last forever.

1 Peter 5:8-11 *THE MESSAGE*

Keep a cool head. Stay alert. The Devil is poised to pounce, and would like nothing better than to catch you napping. Keep your guard up. You're not the only ones plunged into these hard times. It's the same with Christians all over the world. So keep a firm grip on the faith. The suffering won't last forever. It won't be long before this generous God who has great plans for us in Christ—eternal and glorious plans they are!—will have you put together and on your feet for good. He gets the last word; yes, he does.

1 Peter 5:10 *New Living Translation*

In his kindness God called you to share in his eternal glory by means of Christ Jesus. So after you have suffered a little while, he will restore, support, and strengthen you, and he will place you on a firm foundation.

About the Author

Surviving an Amish childhood of abuse and control, the author found herself out on her own at seventeen. She overcame many obstacles to pursue her education without family support. The Amish religion limited her to an eighth grade education forcing her to get her GED before continuing her education. She graduated from a community college with an Associate of Science in Nursing and from an online university with a Bachelor of Science in Nursing. She is a licensed RN, serving patients in a hospital setting.

She struggled to find her identity in other people and things until she found the Lord. She offers hope to all those who suffer and believes the Lord Jesus Christ is trustworthy and places her hope in Him and His Word.

Resources

Books

Amen, Daniel G., *Change Your Brain, Change Your Life*, first edition, 1998.

Chambers, Oswald, *My Utmost For His Highest*, Barbour Books, 1987.

Friesen, J.G., Wilder, J.E., Bierling, A.M., Koepcke, R., Poole, M., *The Life Model: Living From the Heart Jesus Gave You*, Shepherd's House, Inc., 1999.

Moore, Beth, *So Long Insecurity*, Tyndale House, 2011.

Siegel, Daniel J., *The Developing Mind*, The Guilford Press, first edition, 1999.

Music

Ortega, Fernando, *This Bright Hour*, WORD Music, 1998.

Casting Crowns, *"Praise You in this Storm,"* from the album, *Lifesong*, Reunion Records, 2005.

Made in the USA
San Bernardino, CA
17 November 2014